Hiram Powell

A Treatise on the Intellectual, Moral and Social Man

Hiram Powell

A Treatise on the Intellectual, Moral and Social Man

ISBN/EAN: 9783337375324

Printed in Europe, USA, Canada, Australia, Japan

Cover: Foto ©Suzi / pixelio.de

More available books at **www.hansebooks.com**

A TREATISE

ON THE

INTELLECTUAL, MORAL AND SOCIAL

MAN,

WRITTEN UNDER FORTY CAPTIONS.

WITH AN

ESSAY ON MAN,

EMBRACING FIFTEEN HEADINGS OR CAPTIONS,

By HIRAM POWELL.

> "Seize upon truth wherever found,
> On Christian or on heathen ground,
> Among your friends, among your foes,
> The plant's divine where'er it grows."

CINCINNATI:
ROBERT CLARKE & Co., PRINT,
1871.

SPEAK THE TRUTH.

"Speak the truth, and do not waver;
   Speak it boldly everywhere,
Tho' it may displease or favor
   You with others here or there;
Let your heart in early youth
Act in nobleness and truth.

"Speak the truth, though you're offending
   The profession of a friend;
Speak thou not a lie, pretending
   It is better thus to end
Some shameful gossip flying
By a little act of lying.

"Speak the truth, and speak it boldly,
   In the mansion or the cot,
Tho' to some it seemeth coldly,
   And may never be forgot;
It should matter naught to thee,
So thy soul from sin be free.

"Speak the truth thro' life forever;
   Speak it simply, truly, kind;
Let no one in you discover
   Seeds of misery in mind;
But be noble, be enduring,
In the upward life pursuing."

CONTENTS.

PART I.

CHAPTER		PAGE
	Preface	7
I.	Read the Best Books	9
II.	Rich and Poor—The Sources of Wealth and Poverty	12
III.	Aristocracy	19
IV.	Village Aristocracy	23
V.	The Other Side of the Picture	29
VI.	Proposal of a Basis	32
VII.	Faith and Knowledge	36
VIII.	Purposes of Life and the Principle of Morals	41
IX.	The Moral Law	48
X.	Obedience to the Laws of Nature Promotes Happiness	59
XI.	Liberality of Sentiment—Cheerfulness—Happiness	69

PART II.

AN ESSAY ON MAN.

I.	His Mind and Senses—Result of Organization	77
II.	His Nature is ever the Same	83
III.	His Positive and Self-Knowledge	87
IV.	His Education	99
V.	His Moral Accountability	108
VI.	His Personal Freedom	112
VII.	His Self-Improvement	115
VIII.	His Self-Respect and Life-time Duties	120
IX.	His Social Rights and Duties	124
X.	His Peculiarities and Varieties	129
XI.	His Moral Evil	132
XII.	His Penalties	135
XIII.	His Actions are the Results of Circumstances	140
XIV.	He is Held in the Arms of Necessity Forever	148
XV.	His Conflicting Elements and Opposing Forces Harmonized	154

PART III.

CHAPTER		PAGE
I.	Position and Privilege of Truth Speakers	165
II.	Origin and Nature of Government—Of Society	172
III.	Of the Sense of Justice—Of Remorse and of the Consciousness of Merit	181
IV.	Philosophy	186
V.	Nature and Nature's Works	189
VI.	Social Reform—Circumstances	199
VII.	Thoughts on Prejudice	204
VIII.	A Sketch of Natural History	201
IX.	Causes of Crime and Treatment of Criminals	215
X.	Punishment for Children	231
XI.	Mothers and their Daughters	238
XII.	Matter and Motion	243
XIII.	Philosophy, Mystery, and Mutation	246
XIV.	Land Monopoly	252
XV.	The Great Atlantic Cable, etc.	269

PREFACE.

IN offering to the public this volume I have no apology to make, for it has been my constant effort to condense into as small a compass as possible the greatest amount of useful and practical knowledge in plain and familiar language; and, after long and tedious labor, am satisfied that I have so far succeeded in this object as to have presented in this book vastly more information in relation to the intellectual, moral, and social man than can be found in any other work of twice its size.

Its author offers it with the hope that his readers will kindly and impartially investigate it with the spirit of a true philosopher, free from all idle tirade or senseless invectives; that they will peruse it, not with prejudice, but with a desire to discover truth; to enlarge, if possible, their store of useful knowledge, and hence to better their condition through life. Let them carefully investigate, analyze, submit to the closest test, every proposition advanced; then, and not until then, will they be prepared to receive and appreciate facts as they exist. Nevertheless, the writer is not so "green" as to expect to please more than a large majority of his readers; to do much more would be a very bad indication, an indication that his labors are worthless. Indeed, he is convinced in advance that his worthy readers will stumble on many propositions or doctrines, which to them will be rather new, novel, and, perhaps, seemingly absurd; but, reader, you should not prejudge—rather peruse again, stop to think, to meditate, to investigate—because there surely will be found nothing wrong only *your want* of a greater familiarity with such subjects, only your want of a better knowledge of natural laws, of first principles.

It is utterly impossible to believe that which we can not *understand* or *comprehend*, although so many intelligent and well-meaning people too often yield a blind credence to this or that theory or doctrine; but such is not reasonable or philosophical belief. Indeed, strictly speaking, it is no belief at all; but that belief or conviction, which is based upon tangible evidence deduced from common-sense experience and sound philosophy, may be depended upon under all circumstances as a sure and safe road to the Haven of Friendship, Love, and Truth.

This volume is devoted to the great laws, principles, and influences which govern man mentally, morally, and socially—which underlie and control all his actions and affections—as its title indicates, than which none are more neglected, none less understood, and yet none more important. They relate to and teach some of the dearest interests of human life, and gather within themselves some of the most useful questions of practical morality and religion. They take us by the hand, as it were, and lead us into the great temple of life, where sacred duties stand ministering around the altar of Human Wisdom, Benevolence, and Greatness.

It is written (in outline) under forty headings or captions, including an essay on Man (of fifteen captions), perhaps the best to be found in the States, and which alone is worth, to almost any person, ten times the cost of this book. And as the author has, for the last thirty years, not only devoted much time and hard study to these subjects, but has also frequently written upon nearly all of them in the way of contributions to various journals, he entertains a confidence that this little donation is written upon true moral, religious, and scientific principles, and in a manner most *definite, clear, concise,* and yet quite illustrative.

It is a rare and rather novel work, containing a great deal of useful and practical information to be found nowhere else, and interspersed with many sentimental and appropriate selections of poetry, well calculated for all classes and ages of men and women, but more particularly for the young and rising generations.

It contains a vast amount of what might be called domestic or social information—of all information the most useful—and which, if properly understood and reduced to practice, would work a happy reformation, morally and religiously, among the people; would enable them to know themselves, and, consequently, to know all mankind; would teach them to know (the great secret) wherein lies their true and best interest—that it lies in living less for ourselves and more for our dear race—that it lies in the universal equality and consequent prosperity and happiness (as nearly as can be) of all the sons and daughters of Adam; would induce them to cultivate peace, friendship, and charity, hence to respect the feelings, interests, opinions, and even prejudices of their neighbors; to the end that our polluted streams of persecution, condemnation, and (moral) execution for mere imaginary wrongs might dry up, might cease to flow; and, finally, that they might make peace with all mankind, and enjoy the life of practical, moral, and religious men and women under all circumstances, the following pages, to the friends *of Science and Progress,* are dedicated by

THE AUTHOR.

GOOD LIFE.

"He liveth long who liveth well—
    All else is but life flung away;
He liveth longest who can tell
    Of true things truly done each day.

"Then fill each hour with what will last,
    Buy up the moments as they go;
The life above, when this is past,
    Is the ripe fruit of life below.

"Sow love and taste its fruitage pure;
    Sow peace and reap its harvest bright;
Sow sunbeams on the rock and moor,
    And find a harvest home of light."

GOOD COUNSEL.

"Seek not to walk by borrowed light,
    But keep unto thine own;
Do what thou doest with thy might,
    And trust thyself alone!

"Work for some good, nor idly lie
    Within the human hive;
And, though the outward man should die,
    Keep thou the heart alive.

"Strive not to banish pain and doubt
    In pleasure's noisy din;
The peace thou seekest for without
    Is only found within.

"If fortune disregard thy claim,
    By worth her slight attest;
Nor blush and hang thy head for shame,
    When thou hast done thy best.

"Disdain neglect, ignore despair,
    On loves and friendships gone;
Plant thou thy feet, as on a stair,
    And mount right up and on!"

THE
INTELLECTUAL, MORAL, AND SOCIAL MAN.

CHAPTER I.

READ THE BEST BOOKS.

Men live for one another more than for anything else, and the fact stands out on the face of society; therefore, their first and highest desire should be to know themselves, and hence to know each other—to learn those great laws, principles, and relations which govern and control the intellectual, moral, social, and religious man. Now to accomplish which, we must read the best books on history, literature, religion, and the various sciences. But much of what is called literature is not worth the reading—in fact, is worse than useless—mere trash and rubbish, creating a morbid, sickly sentimentality which aims at improbabilities; and the reader of such trash naturally imbibes the idea that "something is to turn up," that fortune and honor must be the result of some startling combinations instead of the reasonable conclusion that they are the effect of earnest application, close study, and hard brain work.

Often after the exhaustion of reading such works, the desire is almost irresistible to seek a little recreation in a broomstick ride through the ethereal regions, or a horseback ride to the moon.

But all literature is not to be condemned, for we have considerable which is really valuable, abounding in flights of wit, flowers of thought, and mines of information; we can not give it all up, but we must separate the dross from the gold. True literature is the natural food of the heart and brain, ennobling the mind, and expanding its powers; but false literature feeds the passions and dwarfs the soul.

Reading is fast becoming the channel of information, hence we ought to be careful that no filth darkens the current. We should learn that rare art of discrimination, and not condemn the fruit because poison lurks in the flower; but the disposition to do this is becoming altogether too prevalent, and the sooner this idea becomes obsolete the better for society.

Our literary works should be drawn from nature—so clear and transparent that the mind's eye may look down in it and see the reflection of all the better traits of human nature, and catching the inspiration, press on to higher and nobler duties. That is the best book which your enlightened understanding tells you is *true* and *beautiful*—because in its truth you entrench yourself, while with its beauty you add the decorations—their truth and beauty become a part of yourself.

We must not forget science—must build no wall between it and the people; because scientific knowledge and moral, intellectual, and physical development are natural allies and handmaidens of each other.

Every family library should contain the best histories

of our own and foreign countries, and standard works on physiology, natural, moral, and mental philosophy, the laws of marraige, of entailment, etc., etc.; also, geology, botany, agriculture, astronomy, atmospheric phenomena, etc., etc. Armed with these, the rocks, the plants and flowers, the earth and elements, become our companions; with these as the magic wand, the granite rock finds a tongue, the rose and the myrtle waves a nod of intelligence, the winds whisper of health and prosperity, while the elements thunder their loud response. What a field opens before us with these in our hands! But powerful as they are, they must be accompanied by careful observation and intelligent thought. We must not only read, but think, day and night; must analyze and get to the bottom of every subject; must learn the laws and relations involved—the whys and wherefores.

Books are but the tools, the brain must work; therefore, to read without mature reflection, is like storing a large number of tools to rust and rot for the want of use.

Then let us "read the best books," and reading let us apply, engraft, and enlarge, leaving nothing to decay or corrode on the brain.

CHAPTER II.

RICH AND POOR—SOURCES OF WEALTH, ETC.

In the unequal distribution of wealth, nature has not been so partial as the poor man generally imagines. The difference in the amount of happiness between the two persons depends upon their imaginary and unsatisfied wants. Whoever saw a rich man have *enough?* In the drawing-rooms of the affluent "luxury lies straining its low thought to form unreal wants," which, being too easily supplied, confer little pleasure. Their food is not seasoned with appetite, and indigestion turns it to disease. The wants of the humble are few, natural, and healthy. The bread of the poor man may be hard to get; he may sigh for the hour of repose; but when obtained, mark with what excellent appetite he enjoys them! He has pleasure that wealth can not command, and no costly conserves are so sweet as those that finish his repast. Appetite and digestion wait, and health is the priceless dessert. No gorgeous tapestry that adorns the canopy of luxury can match the rosy dreams that bedeck the couch of the lowly.

"The rich man," says a Chinese proverb, "is a pig incumbered with fat." No figure can be more appropriate. As wealth accumulates, the dread of using it accompanies; generosity fades.

Charity is shut out, and when a trifle is lost how it afflicts the soul! Wealth thus becomes a heavy burden that is dragged along with pain through life, and when at last death comes, how bitter the parting! That the man of wealth does not work, that he is free from care, is a great mistake. The toil of the mechanic or common laborer has its hour of limit, and sound sleep gives him refreshment; but the toil of head work never ceases. The cares and anxieties of the rich haunt their midnight hours and poison sleep. The miserly propensities that grow up with wealth make the rich man, at best, a hard working, ever wakeful watchman, hired at mean wages to guard a treasure which avails him but little. Whoever saw a man made really more happy, more benevolent, more virtuous, by growing rich? What, then, have the poor to envy?

Therefore let no man be ashamed that he has to perform manual labor for a living. Let him only be ashamed of idleness, dishonesty, and bad habits. Let him not be ashamed of a hard hand nor a sunburnt face. Let him only be ashamed of subsisting like a drone upon the sweat and toil of others; and let him always bear in mind, that if there be a high class, it is those who perform useful work for a living, and that the low class are the lazy and the idle. The workingman, conscious of his usefulness, upholds the dignity of his nature by a becoming self-respect that cringes to no superior.

No man is blessed with greater exemption from care, and no hearth brightened with more domestic happiness. The artificer of all that gives pre-eminence to man, the founder of civilization and human glory, he may stand boldly forth a model of the most noble and most useful work of nature upon the earth.

Having discussed the relative merits, usefulness, and advantages existing between the rich and poor, will now inquire where wealth comes from. As follows: If a dealer in dry goods takes an account of his stock of property, a portion of it will be set down as a number of yards of cloth.

Let us examine a piece of this—say a piece of sheeting—and see where the wealth in it comes from.

In the first place, the cotton was raised on a southern plantation. The seed was planted in the ground, and when the plant came, it was plowed and hoed till the cotton was ripe, when it was picked, baled, and sent to market. Now by this process no new matter was created, and it is regarded by chemists and philosophers as a settled fact that matter can not be produced by man. The elements which form the cotton were previously floating in the air or resting in the earth, and all the farmer did was to bring them together in new combinations, by which process he gave them value. After the bale of cotton reached the shipping port, it was placed on board a vessel and sent over the sea to the manufacturer. By this change of location additional value was given to it. The merchant is not only just as really a producer of wealth as the farmer, but he produces wealth in the same way. Both of them give value to matter by changing its location. The manufacturer draws the cotton out into long slender threads and weaves it into a web of cloth; by this change of its form—of its several parts in relation to each other—gives it additional value. It then passes into the hands of the trader, who separates the large quantity into small parcels, convenient for use, and transports them into the neighborhoods where they will be wanted. By thus changing its location and the relation of the several parts to each other, he imparts to it additional value. The trader is a producer of wealth in the same sense as is the farmer or the manufacturer.

There was a time when there was no wealth in the world: it is now to be reckoned by millions of millions; and if we examine each item of it, we shall find that all this wealth has been produced by making changes in the form, or the relation of the parts, or the location of the several articles of which wealth consists. Let us take one more case, that of a ship. A certain value is given to the logs by cutting and transporting them to the saw-mill, changing their location. They receive additional value by being sawn into plank or timber, removing the surplus, changing the relation of their several parts to each other. The transportation to the ship-yard gives them additional value, changing their location. Then cutting away the portions which are not wanted and placing the materials together in the ship, gives them another installment of value. And thus is wealth produced, by changing the form of some material substance or the relation of its several parts to each other, or its location in such a way as to impart value to it.

Now it will be observed that the reason why these changes give value to the material is, that they advance it a step in the process of adapting it to gratify some human want; but if labor is bestowed upon an article in a way not to have this effect, such labor adds nothing to its value, and of course does not increase the wealth either of the laborer or of the world. If the farmer works the whole season to raise a crop which will satisfy no want, his season's labor adds nothing to his own wealth or the wealth of mankind. If a manufacturer makes such changes in the forms of his articles as not to increase their usefulness, he does not, by such changes, add anything to their value or to his own wealth and prosperity. If a merchant purchases hides in Boston and transports them to Buenos Ayres, where they are worth less than in Boston, he not only loses his own money, but diminishes the wealth of the whole world by the operation.

Now, as regards the sources of poverty, there can be no doubt but a great deal of it is produced by causes entirely beyond our control, and I need not specify them in detail, for they will readily occur to every reflecting mind. But still there are some complaints—in fact, there are many complaints—made continually in relation to hard times, the impossibility of paying debts, supporting families, and contributing to benevolent objects, which are rather unreasonable than otherwise. Whether the old proverb is true or not, and I shall not stop now to discuss it, that "the poor are always prodigal," it does seem as if many who make the above complaints are the very persons who are expending every year nearly double what is necessary for *unneces-*

sary and *injurious* articles of meat and drink, saying nothing of other superfluous habits and customs.

They can hardly make out a meal unless four or five varieties of food and a quantum of strong tea or coffee are before them; after which there must be cigars, and perhaps tobacco, and sometimes ardent spirits and other hurtful drinks are indulged in rather freely. Clogged as they are by this needless extra expense, and incapacitated as they must be for the vigorous prosecution of business, by this excess in eating and drinking, it is no wonder that they find it difficult to keep their expenditures within their income. Now if these views be correct, it would seem that if these people would only adopt those rules of diet and drink for themselves and families which experience and common sense point out as best calculated to promote their health and happiness, they would find their temporal concerns astonishingly improved. Instead of complaining of hard times, the difficulty of supporting their families and paying their debts, they would be continually rejoicing that their lot is cast in a part of the world where their facilities for obtaining the comforts, and even the luxuries of life, are unexampled, and where by honest industry and economy, they can not only do this, but obtain a surplus for meeting in a liberal manner the various calls which education, benevolence, and reform make upon their charity; and beside all this, have something handsome left as a reserve for future exigencies.

Is this saying too much, or will it be thought bordering on fanaticism? Let any poor man who reads these lines keep an exact account of what he pays out for articles of consumption that in fact not only do him no good but really injure him, such as tea, coffee, pork, tobacco, with certain other stimulants and luxuries (saying nothing of the foolishness and extravagance of unnecessary apparel), and the sum total will astonish him—will solve the question why there are so many homeless and destitute families—so many honest and well-meaning men who are forever unable to pay their rents and other debts.

Yes, and all such who may chance to peruse these lines will readily admit that I am about right, when I declare that many of the *causes* of *poverty* might be conveniently removed.

CHAPTER III.

ARISTOCRACY.

The principle of aristocracy is founded in the extreme inequality of conditions. No man can be a useful member of society, except so far as his talents are employed in a manner conducive to the general advantage. In every society the produce, the means of contributing to the necessities and conveniences of its members, is of a certain amount; and in every community the bulk at least of its members contribute, by their personal exertions, to the creation of this produce. What, then, can be more reasonable and just than that the produce itself should, with some degree of equality, be shared among them? What more injurious than the accumulating upon a few, comparatively speaking, every means of superfluity and luxury to the destruction, measurably, of the ease and plain but plentiful subsistence of the many?

It may be calculated that the king even of a limited monarchy receives, as the salary of his office, an income equivalent to the labor of thirty or forty thousand men.

The situation which the wise and good man would desire for himself, and for those in whose welfare he was interested, would be a situation of alternate labor and relaxation—labor that should not exhaust the frame, and relaxation that was in no danger to degenerate into indolence. Thus, industry and activity would be cherished, the frame preserved in a healthy tone, and the mind accustomed to meditation and reflection. This would be, measurably, the situation of the whole human family if the supply of our wants were about equally distributed; but ignorance and aristocracy forbids.

Can any system be more unnatural, unjust, and impolitic than that which converts more than half the people into mere working animals, annihilates so much thought, renders impossible so much virtue, and extripates so much happiness?

Yes, it is truly a humiliating and deplorable circumstance that so large a proportion of the people in every country are forced to become, as it were, mere working animals, and thereby deprived of the precious opportunity of properly developing their intellectual, moral, and social faculties; while a minority of inflated aristocrats wallow in unnecessary wealth, living in extravagance, dissipation, and idleness, considering labor disgraceful and the laboring class as an inferior order of beings, when they are, in fact, the more useful and better class—the bone and muscle, the life and salvation, of every country. Yea—

"The noblest men I know on earth
    Are those whose hands are brown with toil;
Who, backed by no ancestral groves,
    Hew down the wood and till the soil;
And win thereby a prouder name
    Than follows the king or warrior's fame.

"The workingmen, whate'er the task,
  Who carve the stone or bear the hod;
They bear upon their honest brows
  The royal stamp and seal of God;
And worthier are their drops of sweat
  Than diamonds in a coronet.

"God bless the workingmen,
  Who rear the cities of the plain,
Who dig the mines, who build the ships,
  And drive the commerce of the main.
God bless them, for their toiling hands
  Have wrought the glory of all lands."

There is no mistake or vice more thoroughly to be deplored on this subject than that persons sitting at their ease and surrounded by all the conveniencies of life, who are apt to exclaim, "we find things very well as they are;" and to inveigh bitterly against all projects of reform as "the myths and romances of visionary men, and the declamations of those who are never to be satisfied." Now, is it well that so large a part of nearly every people, who are natural heirs to a fair portion of the soil and to the produce of their own labor, should be kept in penury, rendered stupid with ignorance and disgustful with vice, perpetuated in poverty and degradation, goaded to the commission of crimes, and made the unhappy victims to the merciless laws which the rich have instituted to oppress them, to starve them, to degrade them, to enslave them, and very often to imprison and execute them, while they themselves commit far greater crimes, but who, with their ill-gotten treasure, generally purchase their ransom; or, which is more common, outwit the laws, and go scot-free to repeat their crimes. Then, would it be sedition to inquire whether this state of things may not be exchanged for a better?

Or can there be anything more humiliating and degrading than for such men, calling themselves "gentlemen," to exclaim that "all is right," merely because they are floating along at their ease, regardless of the misery, degradation, and vice that may be occasioned in the less favored of their worthy race.

These are but some of the disgraceful and fatal effects of our present favorite system of land monopoly, and it does seem almost useless to write, lecture, or preach against it—against such a *great crime—for men are determined not to think.*

CHAPTER IV.

VILLAGE ARISTOCRACY.

In almost every village of much importance, there is, among certain persons who would be considered, or who fancy themselves to be, actually above others, a spirit of pride, or what is called aristocracy, which is certainly one of the greatest evils; and I should be pardoned for calling it one of the greatest curses that can afflict any community. A great deal of it is to be found among those who, in consequence of their overreaching in business, have succeeded in accumulating the greatest amount of wealth. Yes, I say, a great share of it is confined to the rich people of this character; but generally those who have obtained wealth by honest industry are still too honest, too sensible and worthy, to consider themselves above their industrious, honest, but less gifted or less fortunate fellow-citizens. But I believe that far the greater part of this low and foolish pride is confined to people who are measurably poor; such as shackled traders, merchants, grocers, and very many industrious and honest mechanics, who possess, unfortunately, much more vanity than practical intelligence.

Some official and professional distinctions also not unfrequently operate to feed that vanity and self-esteem which conduce to the evil of which I am complaining, while at the same time a good share of those officers and professors are incompetent and otherwise unworthy to enjoy their positions; for I observe that it is a common practice among civil officers to first consider the *interest* of themselves and favorites before that of the public good, dispensing favors around with public money, to secure friends, "to sell calico," creating large debts and liabilities on the people without their consent, and in violation of the laws before them, etc.

And we yet have another class less useful but more to be pitied than the above—men who have no stability and concentration, and but little tact for any literary business, and being, the most of them, too lazy to labor, are obliged to battle around at one little business or another, always hard up for means to keep their poor souls and bodies together. Consequently they contract debts here and there, promising to pay at stated times, but owing to a want of nerve and moral stamina fail to come to time; thus it goes with them from bad to worse, forever promising to pay, but too often never paying, obtaining about the one-half of their living by deception and intrigue, until they finally contract fixed habits of lying and dishonesty—of *dishonesty and lying*. Hence it is obvious that no lazy and trifling man can possibly possess a good character for truth and veracity—that no aristocratical, self-wise, and self-righteous man can possibly be a Christian.

Aristocrats of these descriptions are confined to no party, order, or sect exclusively—their place is always with what happens to be most popular; and were monarchy or Mohametanism looked upon in the localities where they reside as the most popular, they would be loyal monarchists or flaming Mohametans—anything and everything, right or wrong, decent or indecent, just so it is popular and fashionable.

A want of good sense and principle are at the bottom of a love of this kind of popularity and village aristocracy; but such is, at this time, the raging inclination of nearly the one-fifth of all the world, a large proportion of whom are homeless, but enjoying good health and fair wages—labor hard from morn till night, yet foolishly squander the greater part of their income for mere imaginary wants, for empty show and parade, in order to keep pace with other vain and thoughtless people, for rich and costly attire, furniture, ornaments, luxuries, condiments, etc.

Now the one-half of these expenditures could be saved and laid up to secure the real and enduring advantages and comforts of life—to obtain bountiful domiciles, and to educate and outfit their children.

But instead of exercising such wisdom and foresight, they blindly and recklessly hurry on through time as if *old age and want* could never overtake them; they live for no good purpose, forever remaining poor in order to appear rich and fashionable—a pernicious example to their children and to the young and rising generations, dragging them into vanity, extravagance, dissipation, and crime.

But my readers must not suppose from the foregoing remarks that I am opposed to people dressing and living decently and genteelly, for such is not the fact.

Nothing has pleased me more than to see at the churches, the schools, and at all public gatherings, every man, woman, and child attired in a plain, comely, neat, and appropriate manner—in a manner so as not to attract any particular notice, either on account of ostentation or neglect. Indeed, such should be the custom and style everywhere and on every occasion, particularly in the churches and schools; and how much better would it not look to all sensible and benevolent gentlemen and ladies, and would not a great deal more kindness, sociability, and love abound than we now find in our so-called social circles?

Nothing is so odious to me as aristocracy, for it is the infallible evidence of *immoral* and *little* minds; and I regard it as pardonable to look with pity and contempt on all those who manifest it.

Are not all men of a common parentage and equally free and independent? Should not character, real worth, and public utility constitute the only claim to honor, respect, and distinction? How, then, is it that so many of those who boast of benevolence and justice on their tongues look with a sort of scorn and sovereign contempt upon their more worthier neighbors, merely because they do not exhibit on public occasions so much rich and costly "store clothes"—merely because they may not possess so long a purse, or may not have been so successful in filling it at the sacrifice of other's property? It is because they are really unwise, self-inflated, and vicious, possessing in their souls but litttle true honor, love, and humanity. Such men are not, practically, friends to themselves, to society, to their race, or to the genius of our social institutions; they do not believe, or will not allow, that all men are (in the sight of their Creator) equally useful and worthy. Perhaps their fathers were rich, and this has made them a higher order of beings than their fellows; or, by their boldness and impudence, they have succeeded in attracting more of the gaze and astonishment of the multitude, and this would make it disgraceful in them to descend to the level of worth and virtue where their neighbors are generally found.

To chastise and correct such people the most effectually, they should never have conceded to them, by the citizens, that claim to superiority which they so much covet.

All good men should so behave toward them as to convince them at sight that they do, in reality, look down upon them with as much pity as they affect to look upon others with contempt.

They seem not to know that all classes are equally necessary in any community; that it requires each and every one with their various occupations to form the great social chain; and that the loss of the lowest or meanest (link) class, so-called, would destroy the whole chain, would wreck society, all civilization; and hence we would soon fall back to the point from whence we started—to savage ignorance and barbarity.

Therefore, it is obvious that all men of every class and occupation merit the sympathy, respect, and support of their fellows; and that all this low and foolish pride or village aristocracy is but the legitimate result of inborn ignorance or of improper education; because we see that all persons of real worth and intelligence possess too much consideration, discretion, and humanity to let themselves down to such a low plane.

It is true that, by a fundamental law of nature, varieties, pecularities, affinities, orders, and distinctions abound throughout all creation; hence it is but natural and right that the same shall exist morally, socially and religiously among men; but all orders and distinctions should be based upon true moral, just, and benevolent principles, upon character, upon intrinsic worth and utility, free from all self-inflation, unkindness, and bigotry so common among very many shallow-pated but aristocratical self-wise and self-righteous people.

CHAPTER V.

THE OTHER SIDE OF THE PICTURE.

It is to be regretted that a difference of opinion on the various subjects should be construed into a cause for enmity and separation among men; for even if it should be more pleasant to associate with persons who agree with ourselves in sentiment, it is certainly more useful to communicate with our opponents.

If we live and converse with those only who live and believe as we do, we are very apt to fly into extremes, by pushing our own views and principles beyond the lines of demonstration and prudence; whereas, friendly intercourse with dissenters from our own creed, party, or doctrines corrects the bias of undue partialities and prejudices, and sometimes saves us from errors into which an unreasoning attachment to the offspring of our own imaginations serve to betray us.

Organized parties often strengthen the hands and confirm the hearts of their members; but they also excite their passions and prejudices, and not unfrequently blind their eyes and obscure their judgments to such an extent that they can scarcely see a fault of a brother, but always wide awake to the misgivings of others equally worthy.

Contradiction, if it be not rude or illiteral, is generally

very wholesome; but the intolerant feeling which induces a man to shun the society of those who do not chance to see as he does, deprives him of that very society which, of all others, is best calculated to instruct and improve him.

Like a spoilt child, he is then in great danger of learning to talk nonsense without opposition, of being capricious and extravagant without ever finding it out, his idlest whims and fancies being treated with respect and favor, until he finally mistakes them for infallible truths.

And, in short, for the want of a little correction, argument, and admonition, he is almost certain to lose his modesty and good temper, and ultimately to become a violent, unreasonable, and disagreeable sort of a fellow. Nor must we imagine that this applies only to persons whose opinions may be false and pernicious, but to all men; for no man is unerringly wise, and the very best principles may run up to the seeds of extravagance for the want of proper pruning and culture.

Therefore, however sincerely and positively a man may believe his own opinions true, that is no excuse for refusing to listen and to converse with those whose minds have been differently improved.

If our own creed or convictions should chance to be imperfect or false, we have thus an opportunity to detect their imperfections or discover their falsehood; if they be true and just, we shall at least be warned from extremes, and wavering convictions may be confirmed, and the stamp of reason added to the idle words of belief.

In either case we shall probably become wiser and better, because more tolerant, more moderate, more sociable, and perchance more modest and just beings; and while we may be more thoroughly convinced than before of our own accuracy, we shall, at the same time, be more courteous and reasonable in expressing that conviction.

Let us, then, never shun our adversaries and opponents; for, even if we can not change their sentiments, we may learn to improve and correct and define our own, and should we fail to win their confidence, we may at least secure their good will and respect.

CHAPTER VI.

PROPOSAL OF A BASIS.

ALL the conditions of man and his mental peculiarities are now traced mostly to physical causes and conditions, exhibiting clear and determining laws. The instinct of animals and the mental conditions of men are phenomena exhibited as a consequence of their condition and the influences which have been acting upon them. This is now as clearly understood as the physical conditions and cause of the rainbow and of the thunder-storm. What men are for the most part believing now is a kind of insanity; but, as Bacon says, truly, "Those who resolve not to conjecture and divine, but to discover and know; not to invent buffooneries and fables, but to inspect, and, as it were, dissect the nature of man and the external world, must derive their knowledge from scientific facts and from things themselves."

We know nothing fundamental of nature, nor can we conceive anything of the nature of the primary cause. We know not, nor can we know, what things really are, but what they seem to be to us, and the relations of their appearances. Whatever is, must have a form of being and action. It can not be what it is not, but must be subject to the form or law of its being or constitution. Even suppose the mind was an entity separate from the body, and acting independently of the body, it must still have a nature of its own, and be determined by the form of that nature; and this form of being and action we term law. Nothing can be of itself, or change its condition, unless it be acted upon by something else. A man can not of himself, or by his will, become a tree, any more than a triangle can by any means become a circle; nor are more causes to be admitted than are sufficient to produce any particular change or effect. Hence we require no supernatural causes when we can recognize adequate natural causes inherent in the constitution of nature; and for every effect there is a sufficient cause, and all causes are natural, influenced by surrounding forces and circumstances. I observe that drunkenness and madness, idiotcy, genius, sleep, dreams, charity, are effects, the consequence of our natural condition—of entailment and other circumstances—absolutely and wholly so; for if I pour a bottle of wine down a man's throat, he becomes drunk; and if I press a splinter of bone into the brain, madness ensues; but drunk or sober, mad or idiotic, a man is at all times the result of certain forces and influences.

Some men are, as it were, "a law unto themselves," while others, by their nature, are disposed to thieve and murder. Some men are wolves by their nature, and some are lambs; hence it is vain to talk as if men made themselves what they are, as if entailment and surroundings had no influence over them. But society must be protected from the evil-disposed, and men must be responsible to take the consequences of their acts; but not uncharitably, as if they had selected their own parents, country, education, and surroundings.

Again, if I place a naturally good disposition under favorable circumstances, goodness is invariably the result; whereas, if I place a naturally ill-disposed person under unfavorable circumstances, evil is necessarily the result. We now can perceive precisely why men think as they do; how they are deceived by their own thoughts and feelings; otherwise, their seeming total apathy—their inability to comprehend the nature of science and the necessity of universal law. My greatest desire in life is to acquire knowledge, and a knowledge of human nature in particular—that being the most important and the most needed. And I would freely utter, on all occasions, what I know and believe honestly and without reserve, or the regard for the opinion of a world which is full of superstition and uncharitable prejudice on the one side, while on the other we see the mental powers of men crushed by excessive labor or excessive indolence and indulgence—man everywhere being against his fellow-man.

No moral principle or religious system will elevate men and set them free, except such as is based on a knowledge of causes and the result of a true science of human nature.

This position we may stand upon as on a rock, "and thence observe the wanderings up and down of other men." But I do not wish to dispute with any men about their morals, or their laws of expediency; yet I do say that all the systems of the whole world are very imperfect—they being all founded too much on error—in the ignorance of natural causes—in the ignorance of the great laws of mind; yet, nevertheless, *sufficient for the age*, and should be reverenced none the less. We must exhibit the real fundamental and natural causes of men's thoughts; and out of a knowledge of human nature will grow a wisdom and revelation of principles which will revolutionize the world, and become the guide of man in legislation and education. Let us, then, not assume anything, but "prove all things, hold fast that which is good." Thus may we lay hold of the science of human nature; and until we recognize this science, we shall live in a rude and dark age, and will have but little moral and mental health in us.

CHAPTER VII.

FAITH AND KNOWLEDGE.

"Is it nothing to have faith in nature, to have faith in knowledge and in goodness which is the fruit of knowledge, and which gives us an elevated poetry, gives us the chart and laws of mind to guide us, gives us higher objects for veneration? Is it nothing to have faith in love? Is it nothing to regard nature in all her forms with profound reverence? To have truth and worship goodness, and find no place for contempt of any living thing or condition of matter? Trained in the knowledge of the laws of mind to find it impossible to take offense, to feel a hatred or vindictive spirit toward any living person, however great their offense? What a soothing and happifying influence! What a blessing this one circumstance! What a foundation for virtue and generosity! Is it nothing to cast away vain ambition and to desire true excellence? To feel a noble contentment in reflecting that we are a part of nature—a form of the eternal? Is there nothing in that *faith* which seeks for happiness out of self, in the happiness of others and the glories of nature? I have watched the influence and working of men's faith, and learned to estimate their prejudices and habits of mind, and the force of the different weights which balance and move their thoughts; and when men disparage one another, and bluster about as champions of faith, wisdom, and piety, we may know what is going on—"by what string the puppet has been moved"—and he ceases to have power over me. I can not be moved except by the force of reason and justice, and the example of a disinterested life. It is the light of truth which should guide our steps; it is the warmth of goodness which must develop the latent good that is in us. How *little they* who are pleased to represent human nature as entirely selfish—that even goodness is a selfishness! How little they understand the laws of mind, and how, for instance, the impulse of benevolence, the love of truth, or the sense of beauty, is wholly independent of selfishness. Of course, as a part of nature, as a creature of necessity—of entailment and education, as governed by law—man is neither selfish nor unselfish, neither good nor evil, worthy nor unworthy; but simply nature and what is possible to nature, and could not be otherwise, yet responsible for all his acts.

"The world is full of insane doctrines and customs, fashioned in our ignorance, and each thinks that he can see the insanity and corruption of his neighbors, but can not see his own. The restless and craving absurdity of human wisdom may truly be called vain philosophy. Men are taught logic; but it would seem to be the most useless invention, seeing that they afterward believe in the most illogical conclusions. They are taught, in fact, to believe in what is intellectually most absurd and monstrous, and morally vicious and most barbarous—are taught to proscribe, slander, condemn, and execute, without investigation, their more worthy neighbors; and that for mere imaginary wrongs.

"We must speak out the truth that is within us, even though we shall offend our mother or sister, or our dearest friend; for we live not for the past, but for the future. A man is loved for his virtue so long as his virtue gives no offense to the prejudices, vanities, or vices of the self-wise and self-righteous.

"The reformer must disturb the opinions of many, and he is a demon and robber, and breaks into men's habits and robs them of the opinions which may have been their stay, their character, their wealth, child, and idol.

"Until the philosophy of human nature be admitted among the sciences, and laws and material conditions of mind understood, it seems to me that we are little removed from the pagans, and are still living in the dark ages."

HAVE FAITH.

"Have faith and worry not for to-morrow,
    Leave things of the future to fate;
Never best to anticipate sorrow,
    Life's troubles come never too late.
If to hope over much be an error,
    It is one which the wise have preferred,
And how often have hearts been in terror,
    By fearing what never occurred.

"Have faith and thy faith shall sustain thee;
    Permit not suspicion and care,
With invisible hands to enchain thee,
    But bear what God giveth to bear.

> By his Spirit supported and gladdened,
>   Be ne'er by forebodings deterred;
> But think how oft hearts have been saddened,
>   By fearing what never occurred.
>
> "Have faith and worry not for to-morrow;
>   Short and dark as our life may appear,
> We may make it still shorter by sorrow,
>   Still darker by folly and fear.
> Half our troubles are half our invention,
>   And often from blessings conferred
> Have we shrunk, in the wild apprehension
>   Of fearing what never occurred."

—Romancing rather than using our "gift of reason."

We exhibit our fine fabrics to all the world; but of the fabric of the mind we know but little: and stranger still to say, we do not seem to care to know much. We follow our crude notions and blind instincts like a very worm that crawls, rather than walk erect in true manhood and the light of knowledge. We neglect the true prerogative of man, to know himself, and to guide himself by that knowledge. We try to frighten men to good behavior, and endeavor to patch up grievances, and the last thing we appeal to is the law and authority of nature herself. As knowledge advances, step by step, the world falls back upon precedents and parchments, endeavoring to shut out the light and ruin the philosophy; and the noblest benefactors of their race have been scoffed at in the streets, and hunted out of their country, like poor Windsor, for his gas-lighting, who, escaping with his life, died in poverty abroad. It will be long, I fear, before there is any efficient and general system of training and education, and men fully recognize the fact that the interest of each is in the advancement of the whole, and that the many are not to be sacrificed for the selfish aggrandizement of the few. ATKINSON, F. G. S.

PROGRESS.

"Steadily, steadily, step by step,
Up the venturous builders go,
Carefully placing stone on stone;
Thus the loftiest temples grow."

CHAPTER VIII.

PURPOSES OF LIFE, AND THE PRINCIPLE OF MORALS.

> "Oh! what were life's dull transient hour,
> Without its sunshine and its shower;
> Its day of gloom, and doubt's dark dream,
> And hope's succeeding, brightening beam?"

I BELIEVE that human life rightly understood and rightly used is a beneficient gift, and that it can be so understood and used.

It is irreconcilable to reason that man comes into this world only to suffer and to mourn; it is from his own ignorance, folly, or errors that he does so. He is capable of informing himself, and the means of doing this are, generally, in his power; and if he were truly informed, he would not have to weep over his follies and transgressions.

It is not contended that every one can escape at once from a benighted condition, and break into the region of light, reason, and good sense. But it is most clear from what is well known to have transpired in the world, that each generation may, and have, improved upon the preceding one; and that each individual, in every successive period of time, may better know the true path from perceiving how others have gone before him.

There can be no miracle in this; and it will, at best, be a slow progress; and the wisdom attained in one age, must command the respect of succeeding ones, and receive from them the melioration which they can contribute.

We understand nothing of what is called the perfectibility of human nature, but we understand this, that if human nature can be made to know wherein its greatest good consists, it may be presumed that this good will be sought and obtained. Man was formed on this principle, and he acts on this principle, although he is seen so frequently to make the most deplorable and distressing mistakes; hence if it be not admitted that mankind will always strive to obtain whatsoever seems to them good, and strive to avoid whatsoever seems to them evil, then of course their moral teaching is in vain. If this principle be admitted, the sole inquiry is, what is good and what is evil?

These terms are defined in another part of this work in the following manner: The terms *good* and *evil* are merely relative; the same as up and down; up at one time being down at another, and *vice versa*. But all acts which are most necessary and fitly, producing the greatest good to the greatest number, *present* or *future*, may be called good or necessary, and *vice versa*.

Now the history of the theory of morals, or of practical philosophy, comprises hardly anything but a description of the continuous attempts that have been made to answer also the following questions: By what quality of the mind are we led to form moral distinctions? What is that highest and fundamental principle which regulates and is implied in every mode of virtuous or moral action?

I propose to pass in review the most celebrated theories which have been offered in answer to the latter question. It has at all times been found desirable, and the best interests of society seem to demand it, that the foundation of morals should depend on an immutable and well-defined principle, from which can be deduced every law, maxim, and precept of duty and obligation.

The Principle of Individual Happiness or Rational Self-Love.

Whatever difference of opinion there may prevail with regard to the notion of happiness, all seem to agree in opinion that the consciousness of the agreeable forms its essence. It is undeniable that we ought and have a right to seek and promote our happiness, and that eventually our happiness can only be secured by the practice of virtue—(Epicurus). We can hardly imagine a more powerful motive of human actions than this native, ever present, and irresistible desire of wellbeing. But in order to derive a fundamental and comprehensive principle of morals from the universality and force of this desire, it would first be necessary to convince all mankind that only the sensation of a certain class of pleasurable feelings are worthy to be enjoyed. There is such a great diversity in the conception of happiness, not only among different individuals, but also in the same persons at various times and under various conditions, that it were a hopeless task to propose moral maxims, on the strength of this principle, for general adoption.

Virtue and happiness are not identical ideas. Common sense makes an easy distinction between the consciousness of inner worth or moral dignity and the sensation and satisfaction of the agreeable. To be virtuous is something more than being happy, even in popular estimation. If happiness be limited to the feeling of that serenity and elevation of mind which consists in discharging to the best of our knowledge and power all the duties in the various relations of life, and to the proper development and exercise of all our mental and bodily functions, it were still inadequate to become the principle of the whole of morals, for virtue is nevertheless something more yet than all this.

Many a virtuous man is sustained under the load of misery and wretchedness which destiny had in store for him, by the bracing influence of conscious innocence and rectitude, but who would smile bitterly at the imputation of his happy state and condition. I esteem and admire such a man, but envy not his fate.

The Principle of the Greatest Good to the Greatest Number.

The moral maxim which flows from this principle requires that we should invariably prefer the welfare of the many to that of the few, in order to obviate the clash of duties, to harmonize the functions of justice, and thereby produce the greatest amount of happiness.

This principle includes, at the most, only a very small part of morals, and sets up a rule which measures actions according to their extensive and not intrinsic worth; and it is also more plausible than just, and however noble it sounds, and undoubtedly useful it is, as a subordinate principle of morals, yet designing men and despots have commonly resorted to it, and much to the injury of society.

The Principle of General Benevolence.

That quality of the mind which greatly exercises its functions for the promotion of the general good, and engages its benign influences for the real happiness of others, is certainly a fruitful source of virtuous deeds—(Hutcheson). But it is impossible to formulate a moral maxim, on the basis of general benevolence, which pays regard to all the diversified duties of life.

Considerations of utility and fitness of things must greatly enter into its construction, to make it available for a fundamental and unexceptional principle of morals.

The Principle of Utility—(Helvetius).

A vast number of social and public virtues originate from a knowledge of their usefulness, and it may be safely asserted that the exercise of morality is never without its accompanying utility. It is, however, far from being true that moral approbation is uniformly elicited by considerations of the usefulness of virtuous actions.

Many praiseworthy efforts can not be attributed to a motive which postulates itself on self-love.

The Principle of Truth—(Wollaston).

The moral maxim derived from this principle prescribes that our will should at all times act in conformity to the laws of truth, as established in the nature of things and their relations. According to this principle, every sin or transgression is the effect of ignorance or of an error of judgment, and every improvement in character marks a step in the advancement of knowledge.

It is nevertheless always dangerous to make morals dependent on a general theory of truth, for this itself requires an exposition which experience has shown is not calculated to produce the desired unanimity of acquiescence—(The Stoics, Academicians). Nor is it universally true that man is vicious only on account of his ignorance and false reasoning, for persons frequently sin against their better knowledge and conscience, being controlled by their excessive appetites and passions.

The Principle of the Harmonious Development of all the Qualities of our Nature to their utmost Degree of Perfection.

A number of excellent moral maxims may be deduced from this principle as a means of securing individual and social happiness; but it were a delusion to imagine that because we can group everything that is good under the head of perfection, that we have thereby really found the highest and most comprehensible moral principle, for it may be asked what becomes of those duties which oblige us to practice a self-denial not always short the sacrifice of life itself? I may answer that reason justifies, and that the good of our race frequently calls for it, and that those who voluntarily give their lives for their kind, perform the highest moral act known to humanity.

CHAPTER IX.

THE MORAL LAW.

This is a subject of vast importance, and to investigate it properly we must not only take common sense, reason, and experience for our guide, but we must also keep in view those great laws and principles which underlie and control the actions of men. The Moral Law is that power which controls and governs the actions, affections, and mental intercourse of men. It is the basis of all good governments, good society, and true religion; but which is, nevertheless, shamefully neglected—scarcely ever spoken of; no, not even from the pulpit. True moral action consists in the exercise of benevolence, justice, and equality, in being not only useful to ourselves, but in doing all in our power to improve the condition of others.

We believe that the material world is governed by inexorable laws, which can not be violated or suspended; and that intellectual beings are in like manner subjected to laws—the physical, intellectual, moral, and social—and that they have learned, more or less perfectly, what these laws are, and their nature and purposes. That in all the term of life possessed by each individual, he is under the necessity of doing certain acts for himself and relatively for those with whom he is associated by family ties and by social bonds.

That he ought to abstain from acts which are injurious to himself and others, and from acts which disturb the good order and harmony of the political association of which he is necessarily a member.

Now if we so believe, then such belief should be followed by the conviction that we must learn and conform to the rules and precepts which are adapted to accomplish these ends of our being.

Morality, then, lies not only in knowing its laws, rules, and precepts, but particularly in conforming to them. In the proportion in which these rules and precepts are known to us, and observed by us, we shall conform to the object of our being as discernible in nature; and in the proportion in which we are uninstructed in these laws and precepts, or disobedient to them, we shall fall short of obtaining the good of which we are capable of promoting our true and best interest.

But in what manner does nature urge and command us to seek our true and best interest and preservation?

By two powerful and involuntary sensations which she has attached as two guides or guardian powers to all our actions; the one, the sensation of pain, by which she informs us of and turns us from whatever tends to our injury and destruction; the other, the sensation of pleasure, by which she attracts and leads us toward everything that tends to our benefit and preservation.

But sometimes they deceive us in two ways—through our ignorance and our passions. They deceive us through our ignorance, when we act without knowing the effect of objects on our senses; for instance, when a man handles nettles without knowing their quality of stinging. And they deceive us through our passions when, though we are acquainted with the hurtful action of objects, we notwithstanding give way to the violence of our desires and appetites; for example, when a man knows that wine inebriates, drinks nevertheless to excess.

Now what results from these facts? The result is, that the ignorance in which we enter the world, and the inordinate appetites to which we give ourselves up, are opposed to our best interest and preservation; that, in consequence, the instruction of our minds, and the moderation of our passions are two obligations, or two laws immediately derived from the first law of preservation.

Yes, ignorance and willful disobedience are the causes of nearly all the immorality, suffering, and crime among men; hence the vast importance of teaching our children to know something of themselves—something more than is taught in our fashionable schools.

But all those who are well instructed in the moral law, in mental science, are favored with a monitor under the name of conscience, which seldom fails in that case to perform the duties of its office; yet this "conscience" is mostly a thing of education, and operates well or ill, usefully or mischievously, according to the character of the mind in which it resides; hence it is but a fallacious and precarious guide.

As above stated, morality consists not only in knowing its laws and precepts, but more particularly in the practice of them; therefore, all men in every department of business should be governed by true moral principles. All civil officers should move firmly forward in the discharge of their sacred duties, adopting the law, justice, and equality as their only rule of action, knowing not their own private interest nor one man or district above another.

They should never purloin or use public funds for private purposes, to secure friends, "to sell calico;" nor give aid or countenance in forwarding clandestine and illicit schemes gotten up by unholy factions.

All merchants, druggists, grocers, etc., should deal fairly and equally with their patrons, giving good weights and measures, never offering for sale any damaged goods or other articles, only at reduced prices; for if *they purchase damaged goods or other property, the fault is their own*, hence their customers *should not be swindled* on that account. And because, also, the moral law presumes that all traders know their business, and consequently holds them guilty of *fraud* for all its violations.

All mechanics should do their work honestly and faithfully, receiving no more than a fair consideration for the same, and never allowing work and jobs badly executed to go out of their shops only as such and at reduced prices; for the moral law presumes that they, too, understand their business, and therefore should not swindle their customers.

All farmers should deal honestly in the sale of their produce and stock, never offering in market any damaged or unwholesome meats, breadstuffs, or other articles; nor sell a horse or milch cow without giving the purchaser all their bad qualities as well as their good ones. Nor should they ask for a horse, cow, or other property more than a fair consideration, because all they receive above a fair price—above what they themselves consider the true worth—is *fraudulently obtained* and a departure from the moral law.

But the great majority of farmers, merchants, and traders will demur against all this kind of philosophy, and excuse themselves by replying that every man's eyes must be his own market; that other people do not deal with them on such principles, and therefore they can not afford to do it. True ; yet all this amounts to nothing—mere sophistry; for, with the same propriety, they might say that because other men lie, cheat, and steal to defraud them, that they have a moral right to do the same.

Again, no man in any business should ever tell a falsehood to effect a sale, a swap, or to avoid paying a debt, because in so doing he not only outrages the moral law, but debases himself below his race. He thereby acknowledges, in silent language, that he is too *ignorant* and *onery* to make a living without lying—*without lying.*

All such weak and deluded mortals, of whom we have legions, are an annoyance to any community—an enemy, practically, to themselves and to their own best interest; but all good and intelligent men will pity such, and feel very thankful that they are not also mean like them, because they are either the incestuous offspring of incompatible alliances or of perverted and corrupt education and surroundings. Born, perhaps, of ignorant, rude, and vicious parents, consequently inheriting by entailment more or less of their evil qualities; but if not from them, then from remote and like ancestry; hence it would be unnatural for them to act differently from what they do; yet, notwithstanding, we should chastise them, in mercy, when we *must*—for their reformation and the good of society.

And we yet have another class, many of whom are tip-top gentlemen, but who, nevertheless, seem to think so little of themselves and of society, as to be frequently seen on the sideways and in public places, chewing their quids, puffing a cigar, or swinging a great pipe from their teeth, patronizing beer and lemonade saloons, if nothing worse.

All this fashionable rudeness is very ingenious and demoralizing to any community, because our boys are, as they should be, creatures of imitation; and hence it is but natural for them to follow such pernicious examples—but natural for them to imitate the better class of society.

It is, then, no wonder that we have so many boys who are "men," chewing and smoking the nasty weed, drinking beer, ale, lemonade, whisky, etc., etc.; then it is no wonder that we have so many inebriates, loafers, gamblers, robbers, etc.; nor is there any hopes of much reformation in that direction so long as fathers—the respectable fathers and church members who shape society—continue to hold out to the young and rising generations such immoral and seductive examples.

Now, as the majority of my readers use tobacco in some way, and perhaps very many of them consider the use and example as rather harmless, and only a matter which should concern themselves, I will here, for their benefit, quote part of a lecture delivered recently by I. C. Jackson, M. D., in Danville, New York:

"Of all narcotic substances used as condiments or for appeticious purposes, tobacco presents the most objectional features. This poisonous substance is a most powerful narcotic. It stupefies the brain, while at the same time it depresses the heart's action. Begun to be used in early life, it creates such a condition of the circulation of the blood and of the nervous fluids, as to render its subject strongly predisposed to the use of alcoholic stimulus. I never knew but one besotted drunken man who was not a user of tobacco, though I have known a great many who have used tobacco who were not drunken men. I never knew a tobacco chewer who did not use some form of stimulus. Pledged as many tobacco chewers are to total abstinence from alcoholic drinks as a beverage, they are shrewd and sagacious in the use of some form of stimulant. For instance, I have never yet known a tobacco chewer who, unless prohibited by a physician, did not casually or habitually drink tea; nor have I ever known one who did not use with his food largely and freely the condimental spices. Some of these are very powerful stimulants, reacting against the depressing effects of tobacco, together with which they create habitual conditional or functional states that strongly predispose the subject to the use of alcoholic stimulants, which are stronger and more effective in the production of reactionary results than themselves are.

"Where a man uses tobacco and drinks no tea nor coffee, nor uses any of the exciting spices in his food which are common as condiments on our tables, I hold it to be almost physically impossible for him not to use alcoholic drinks as a beverage. The only alternative against their use is the abandonment of tobacco. I believe in this; the more observing and widely experienced physicians will concur with me; because they understand that *stimulants* and *narcotics*, or *exaltants* and *depressants*, necessarily antagonize each other.

"He who constantly depresses his heart's action by the use of a poison, like tobacco, will feel that he needs a stimulus to overcome that depression.

"Again, some years ago, it was ascertained by the then acting chaplain of the New York State prison at Auburn, that not less than seven-eighths of the convicts had committed their crimes when in a state of intoxication; and that three-fourths of that seven-eighths admitted that the provoking and most powerful cause of their past intemperance was the use of tobacco.

"They first learned to use it, and under its use to drink liquor, and when intoxicated by liquor they committed crime."

Then do not the foregoing illustrations prove most conclusively, that our respectable fathers and tip-top gentlemen are mostly to blame for all the vice, dissipation, and crime in any community; and do they not also prove most clearly that not less than the one-half of all our inebriates are produced by the free use of tobacco.

Now having treated this subject much farther than

was anticipated, must come to a close; but will fain hope that my readers will give the above suggestions and strictures some little attention; because if we know not those great principles and precepts of the moral law, how can we live in obedience to them; how can we be uniform and practical, moral or religious men unless we know how to be such—unless we know ourselves—the great laws of mind, with those agencies and influences which underlie, govern, and control all the actions and affections of men?

If we can, then the ancient Catholics were moral and religious men when they were persecuting, condemning, and burning Protestants merely for opinion's sake; then the Christians of Europe and North America were moral and religious when they were executing by fire, the sword, and the gibbet, hundreds of thousands of innocent women and children for the imaginary crime of witchcraft. Now I am among the first to frankly acknowledge that they were, when committing those outrages, just as honest as the best of us are to-day; but that does not in the least palliate their crimes—does not satisfy the *moral law*.

Men frequently commit great crimes conscientiously, such as robbery and murder, and afterward repent and ask forgiveness; but that does not return the stolen property, nor the life of the murdered man—that does not pay the debt of sin, although it is good for individuals and for society that they so repent, reform, and sin no more. But all our past sins (or wrongs) must be atoned for, sooner or later, by the first to the fourth generation. For instance, the Americans lived happily and prosperously for many generations while reveling in the great sin of slavery; and finally millions of them repented and asked forgiveness for their past crimes; but the day of retribution had to come.

Their ship was unsound, the crew mutinous, the winds blew, and the angry waves beat hard against her—to the bottom she went, carrying down with her about six hundred thousand valuable lives and thousands of millions of treasure. "Truly the way of the transgressor is hard."

Therefore, it is good for us to suffer in due time for all our foolish and bad conduct, because every chastisement we receive for crime—for disobeying laws—makes us that much wiser and better; and also cautions our neighbors that they may avoid the like mistakes; and because, also, *wisdom consists in knowing the law, and virtue and piety in living in obedience to them*—and *vice versa*.

Consequently, it is impossible for any of us to live *uniform* and practical, moral or religious men and women only by *knowing* and living in obedience to the laws of our *being* and of society. And strange to tell! that more than eighty per cent. of all the adult inhabitants of the earth are to a great extent morally and socially, like little children, who love one another, yet when together, *as they must be,* do not know how to treat each other. Hence very soon troubles and contentions arise—all for the want of the knowledge above indicated.

But still children are unlike and vastly more pious than men and women, because they very soon forgive and love one another as well as ever; because their innocent and generous souls have not yet been *educated* to hate and bear malice and vengeance; because their little bosoms have not yet become the unclean abode of demons.

And lastly, if we would really esteem and love ourselves, and hence promote our own best interest—would have our neighbors respect us—would wear an honest countenance, and enjoy the rich blessings of a cheerful and happy disposition, we must possess *wisdom*, and exercise every day kindness, indulgence, veracity, justice, and fair dealing with all men.

CHAPTER X.

OBEDIENCE TO THE LAWS OF NATURE PROMOTES HAPPINESS.

THERE is, perhaps, no word in our language more commonly used, nor any one less defined or less understood than the term *happiness*. It is sometimes taken to mean pleasurable sensations derived from the gratification of the appetite; sometimes it means a peculiar state of the mind. Murderers, when they are about to be swung from the gallows, are often represented as happy; because they committed such odious crimes they were sinners, and supposed themselves bound to perdition. But, after they had murdered, repented of their sins, and confidently expected to go to heaven; hence they were quite happy. Such are some of the ideas that men entertain of happiness. Perhaps it is easier to tell what happiness is *not*, than what it *is*. The most perfect health can hardly be called happiness, unless one has something to do, and takes delight in doing it. Health and riches do not, as a general thing, make men happy.

These accidents of being rather excite cravings for enjoyment, and lessen benevolence and general friendship.

They are means, not ends. A rich man can ride but one horse, or sit in but one coach, or eat but one dinner, or wear but one suit of garments, or live but in one house *at a time;* and persons of moderate circumstances can do the same. Health, riches, power, and distinction do not make happiness, for distinction is troublesome—it has more pains than pleasures. It is jealous, envious, and distrustful. Power does not make men happy, for it demands the most busy watchfulness to keep it. Riches are the means of enabling men to live in elegance and luxury, and even, as is very common, in voluptuous enjoyment. But this is no way to be happy, for the appetite soon becomes satiated. The stomach wears out, and the senses are palled—diseases come. The body may be sorely racked on a velvet couch as well as on a straw bed.

Is there, then, any such thing as happiness? There must be such a thing, or the laws of nature, which provide for physical, intellectual, and moral being, are false and deceitful, and the gift of reason is a fable. If there be such a thing as happiness, *it will be found in that knowledge of and obedience to the laws of nature and society, which makes health, longevity, wisdom, and all there is of us in this world.*

It will be found in obeying the propensity to action to some continuous, useful end; that is, in pursuing, in a reasonable and honorable manner, some one of the many vocations in society, which tend to secure one's own self-respect, comfort, and peace of mind, and which tend, also, to the common good. Such as any honest manual or intellectual labor which advances the good of society; or the sale and merchandise of all articles of trade which the people, for their growth, education, sustenance, and general prosperity in all the departments of business really need; and such, and such only. Hence the sale of ardent spirits and of all other drinks as a beverage—the sale and merchandise of tobacco, opium, etc., as a beverage, in any shape whatever—must be considered really immoral and illegitimate—as entirely useless and quite pernicious to the physical, moral, and religious growth of society.

What! who ever heard before of anything wrong in keeping genteel shops for the sale, as a beverage, of beer, ale, cider, soda-water, lemonade, etc.? I am sure such drinks can do no harm! The writer must be a fanatic! "But stop, friends, one story is good until another is told." These are truly the worst of shops; for such (and what are called decent and respectable whisky saloons) are the primary departments in the great school of drunkenness.

In just such, thousands of our good men and boys first whet up their latent appetites; when they can not get beer, cider, etc., to drink, they will hanker and thirst for something stronger (boys must first learn to spell before they read).

It is in such "harmless" shops where men and boys first cultivate the pernicious habit of loafing and lounging—of gabbing all sorts of nonsense and vulgarity, and of fooling away their time, money, and brains.

I tell you what it is, good folks, we want nothing in this line what you call decent, harmless, and respectable. We are down on all this fashionable decency and respectability. If we have to be afflicted with anything of this sort, give us the very lowest and filthiest sinks of iniquity—kept only by the most unblushing men. For such low and disgraceful shops will only be patronized by the very lowest characters, who have not in their constitutions moral stamina enough to ever be reclaimed. Hence we will still retain about all the useful and best material in society. Indeed, such miserable sinks will have a moralizing influence on all observing, decent, and thinking men and boys in any community.

Yet, strange to tell! that so very many intelligent and respectable men, who are self-bound slaves to one or more of these poisonous "luxuries," will excuse themselves by saying, O! I know it is a bad practice and is hurting me, but—but—somehow I've got into the habit of it, and can't quit it. These same men claim for themselves a good share of dignity, love of approbation, moral courage, and intelligence; yet scoff at the science of phrenology, and proudly declare that all men could, if they only would, leave off their bad practices. They also claim a great deal of free agency, when, in fact, their conduct goes to show that they have very little of either. They must not think it strange—must not look about for miracles—if their own sons should drift into the same bad practices, while they, their self-wise and worthy selves, are offering such bad examples to them and to the young and rising generations. Finally, we may feel assured that if *we* so live as to be healthy; so use our time as to be reasonably busy to some good purpose, and so conduct ourselves as to be justly entitled to our own approbation; so cultivate and shape our minds as to *trust in ourselves*—to think for ourselves—to understand ourselves, those laws, relations, and influences which control all our affections and actions; to see things on their right sides and from the proper stand-points; to extract good, present or future, from all circumstances; and hence to exercise charity and indulgence for the misgivings, opinions, and prejudices of others, we will be respectable, prosperous, cheerful, and happy. Then why should you not, in order to be a man, and to feel like a free man—to enjoy through life your full measure of happiness, and finally to render to your Creator a good account of your past stewardship—

TRUST IN YOURSELF.

"You might be a happy elf,
If you could but trust yourself:

1. "Find the wisdom to provide—
Goodness of your own to guide.
You've within you all the light,
Needful in the darkest night;

2. "Learn that wisdom here is wealth,
And you'll be a happy elf.
And in sickness and in health,
Poor or rich may trust yourself;

3. "And in fear, as well as grief,
You will find your own relief.
If you want your soul quite clean,
Do no wrong, and nothing mean;

4. "All the love required of you,
   Is enough to keep you true.
   True to good—to just behavior—
   To yourself—to your neighbor;

5. "Then in living, and in dying,
   You'll be happy, death defying."

I will now make some further remarks in regard to the sources of human happiness, and the conditions requisite for maintaining it. I quote from Dr. Combe's "Constitution of Man:"

"The first and most obvious circumstance which attracts attention is, that all enjoyments must necessarily arise from activity of the various systems of which the human constitution is composed. The bones, nerves, muscles, digestive and respiratory organs furnish pleasing sensations, directly or indirectly, when exercised in conformity with their nature, and the external senses, and internal faculties, when excited, supply the whole remaining perceptions and emotions, which, when combined, constitute life and rational existence. If these were habitually buried in sleep, or constitutionally inactive, life, to all purposes of enjoyment, might as well be extinct. Existence would be reduced to mere vegetation, without consciousness.

"If, then, wisdom and benevolence have been employed in constituting man, we may expect the arrangements of creation, in regard to time, to be calculated, as a leading object, to excite his various powers, corporeal and mental, to activity. This accordingly appears to me to be the case; and the fact may be illustrated by a few examples. A certain portion of nervous and muscular energy is infused by nature into the human body every twenty-four hours, which it is delightful to expend; and to provide for its expenditure, the stomach has been constituted so as to require regular supplies of food, which can be obtained only by nervous and muscular exertion. The body has been created destitute of covering, yet standing in need of protection from the elements; and nature has been so constituted that raiment can be easily provided by moderate exercise of the mental and corporeal powers. It is delightful to repair exhausted nervous and muscular energy by wholesome aliment; and the digestive organs have been so constituted as to perform their functions by successive stages, and to afford us frequent opportunity of enjoying the pleasures of eating.

"In these arrangements the design of supporting the various systems of the body in activity, for the enjoyment of the individual, is abundantly obvious.

"Now directing our attention to the mind, we discover that individuality and the other perceptive faculties desire, as *their* means of enjoyment, to know existence, and to become acquainted with external objects; while the reflecting faculties desire to know the nature, dependencies, and relations of all objects and beings. 'There is something,' says an eloquent writer, 'positively agreeable to all men, to all, at least, whose nature is not most groveling and base, in gaining knowledge for its *own sake*. When you see anything for the first time, you at once derive some gratification from the sight being new; your attention is awakened, and you desire to know more about it. If it is a piece of workmanship, as an instrument, a machine of any kind, you wish to know how it is made, how it works, and what use it is of. If it is an animal, you desire to know where it comes from, how it lives, what are its dispositions, and generally its nature and habits. This desire is felt, too, without at all considering that the machine or the animal may ever be of the least use to yourself practically, for, in all probability, you may never see them again. But you feel a curiosity to learn all about them, because they are new and unknown to you. You accordingly make inquiries; you *feel a gratification* in getting answers to your questions—that is, *in receiving information*, and in knowing more—in being better informed than you were before. If ever you happen again to see the same instrument or animal, you find it agreeable to recollect having seen it before, and to think that you know something about it. If you see another instrument or animal, in some respects like, but differing in other particulars, you find it pleasing to *compare them together*, and to note in what they agree, and in what they differ. Now, all this kind of gratification is of a pure and disinterested nature, and has no reference to any of the common purposes of life; yet is is a pleasure—an enjoyment. You are nothing the richer for it; you do not gratify your palate, or any other bodily appetite; and yet it is so pleasing that you would give something out of your pocket to obtain it, and would forego some bodily enjoyment for its sake. The pleasure derived from science is exactly of the like nature, or, rather, it is the very same.' This is a correct and forcible exposition of the pleasures attending the active exercise of our intellectual faculties; but to reap happiness in the greatest *quantity* and maintain it *most permanently*, the faculties must be gratified *harmoniously*. In other words, if among the various powers, the *supremacy* belongs to the moral sentiments, then the aim of our habitual conduct must be the attainment of objects suited to gratify them. For example, in pursuing wealth or fame, as the leading objects of existence, full gratification is not afforded to benevolence, veneration, and conscientiousness, and consequently complete satisfaction can not be enjoyed; whereas, by seeking knowledge, and dedicating life to the welfare of mankind and obedience to the laws of our Creator, in our several vocations, these faculties will be gratified, and wealth, fame, health, and other advantages will flow in their train, so that the whole mind will rejoice, and its delight will remain permanent.

"Again, to place human happiness on a secure basis, the laws of external creation themselves must accord with the dictates of the moral sentiments, and intellect must be fitted to discover the nature and relations of both, and to direct the conduct in harmony with them.

"Much has been written about the extent of human ignorance; but we should discriminate between absolute incapacity to know, and mere want of information arising from not having used this capacity to its full extent. In regard to the first, or our capacity to know, it appears probable that we shall never know the essence, beginning, or end of things; because these are points which we have no faculties calculated to discover. But the same Creator who made the external world constituted our faculties, and if we have sufficient data for inferring that his intention is that we shall enjoy existence here while living, and if it be true that we can be happy here only by being conversant with those natural laws which, when observed, are pre-arranged to contribute to our enjoyment, and which when violated visit us with appropriate suffering, we may safely conclude that our mental capacities are wisely adapted to the attainment of these objects, whenever we shall do our own duty in bringing them to their proper condition of perfection, and in applying them in the best manner.

"Now, if the intention of our Creator be that we should enjoy existence while in this world, then He knew what was necessary to enable us to do so, and He will not be found to have failed in conferring on us powers fitted to accomplish His design, provided we do our duty in developing and applying them.

"The great motive to exertion is the conviction that increased knowledge will furnish us with increased means of happiness and well-doing, and with new proofs of benevolence and wisdom in the great Architect of the Universe."

> "Then ye fathers, pray do your part,
> And teach your children right to know;
> When they're old they'll not depart,
> If trained the way they ought to go.
>
> "Your child was given you to rear,
> In ways of honesty and truth;
> But ah! too plainly doth appear
> The sheer neglecting of the youth."

CHAPTER XI.

LIBERALITY OF SENTIMENT—CHEERFULNESS—HAPPINESS AND MISERY.

So great is the weakness of human nature, and such is the force of prejudice, that there are men who are liberal in some things and not in others. Where the passions are strongly excited, where the prejudices and partialities are great, men the most liberal in other respects, suffer themselves to be led away without examination, and from the implicit faith which they attach to certain opinions, think themselves justified in reprobating all those who differ from them, and, contrary to the mildness of their nature, use a degree of severity when they speak of such differences, which would seem to indicate a great want of liberality and cool reflection. The good effects of liberal sentiments can never be sufficiently felt and understood till they are contrasted with those of an opposite quality, for such is the constitution both of the natural and moral world, that *virtue and beauty derive their luster from their opposites.*

Illiberality is generally connected with the worst of our passions, and he whose mind is engrossed by any of these, has no consideration or compassion for the feelings, opinions, or the comforts of those who surround him. Ambition, envy, pride, malice, hatred, jealousy, revenge, and avarice are passions which endure no rivals; everything must yield to their gratification, or be sacrificed to their power; the gentle voice of moderation and reason is never heard in their presence; a benevolent feeling for the wants, ignorance, and desires of other people is never experienced for a moment, and he who dares in any instance to oppose their power will feel, whether he deserves it or not, the violence with which they bear down all before them, right or wrong. Whereas, liberality stops to examine the *true state of things, and mildly interprets the motives of others;* but illiberality never deigns to reflect any further than that such and such things are contrary to her opinion or interest.

Illiberality is a lesser sort of tyranny, for the illiberal man wishes all people to think as he does, even in trifles, and where he has the power will compel them to do so. If he is a father, will esteem his children only as they accord with his own sentiments or cease to oppose them; he will pay no attention to their feelings, pleasures, or sentiments, if they differ from his own, and will estimate all their merit by its conformity to his own standard.

Similarity of opinion is often mistaken for liberality of sentiment, and we are apt to conclude that they who think as we do, think liberally; yet this mistake frequently does harm, for it deceives us with the idea of acting with propriety while we are doing exactly the reverse.

The dissenter thinks every churchman must be illiberal, while those of his own persuasion he considers as men of enlarged sentiments, and *vice versa.* Liberality, however, does not consist in a man's own opinions, but in the *tenderness* and *respect* which he shows to those who differ from him; it is not what we think or believe, but what we think of *others*, that makes us deserve the name of liberal; for though freedom from prejudice is one part of liberality, yet to respect the prejudices of others is a greater, and it is certainly that part which mostly contributes to the peace, comfort, and pleasure of society. We are apt, by a very common mistake, to confound indifference with liberality, and a man who has no opinions of his own is often said to be liberal to others— a degree of praise to which he has properly no claim, for the most liberal men are generally the most tenacious and best convinced of their own opinions; and as they feel how much it cost them to arrive at conviction, they pardon with more ease the mistakes and misgivings of others.

And, again, this liberality of sentiment, this charity, respect, and indulgence for the ignorance, wants, and opinions of others, naturally begets in their possessors a cheerful, jocose, and happy disposition; and it is the part of a good man and a true philosopher to jest and be merry as well as to preach; but it is exceedingly tedious and unpleasant to see people budging along through life ever with a frown on their faces, and a sigh on their lips; they become pestilential, and one is apt to catch the malady by contact. Such people don't realize that there is any sunny side to this life of ours; a smile seems to them to be sadly out of place on a companion's face, and a hearty laugh downright blasphemy. O pity, pity, what philosophy! Cheerfulness is an amulet—a charm to make us permanently contented and happy.

A cheerful man feels well, does well, and loves things which are good; while he who is always sad doeth ill in the very sorrow he evinceth. Long-faced, sanctimonious people are generally avoided, and very justly so, for who wishes to partake of their malady? Whereas, those who possess bouyant spirits, and hence look on the sunny side of life, are ever courted for the genial emotions they diffuse about them.

He who administers medicine to the sad heart, in the shape of wit and humor, is most assuredly a good Samaritan, for a cheerful face is nearly as good for an invalid as healthy weather. To make a sick man think he is dying, all that is necessary is to look half-dead yourself! Open unrestrained merriment is a safety-valve to the heart and disposition, because it is a fact beyond dispute that mirth is as innate in the mind as any other quality that nature has planted there; it only wants civilization, and the more we cultivate it the more faithful and useful it becomes.

Mirror-like, the world reflects back to us the picture which we present to its surface; and a cheerful heart paints the world as it sees it, like a sunny landscape, while the morbid mind depicts it like a sterile wilderness; and thus, chameleon-like, life takes its hue of light or shade from the soul on which it rests, dark or sunny as the case may be.

David Hume used to say that a habit of looking on the best side of every event is better than a thousand pounds a year. Bishop Hall quaintly remarks,

"For every bad there might be a worse, and when a man breaks his leg, let him be thankful it was not his neck."

This is the true spirit of submission and resignation—one of the most beautiful and useful traits that can possess the human heart—a strong indication of a manly, noble, and well-cultivated mind. Then resolve to see this world of ours—this beautiful and bountiful world—on its sunny side, and you have about half won the battle of life at the outset.

For cheerfulness and happiness consist only in harmony of the body and mind with nature and society; they are the result of a healthy and well-working system of organization, combined with accordant actions and reactions from nature and society to the perceptions and reminiscences of the brain—the definition leads to its means. Healthy action can result only from temperance in eating and drinking, regularity of habits, cleanliness of person, exercise to promote the circulations, and excitement to exercise. Accordance with nature will result of course, and may be improved by its study; while accordance with society will arise from being truthful, just, sympathizing, benevolent, unostentatious, and useful. Self-satisfaction will result from such a state of personal and external harmony, and all the perceptions of happiness be enjoyed of which humanity is susceptible.

Misery is the result of an unhealthy and ill-working system of organization, or of discordant actions and reactions between nature and society and the individual; it is the body and mind in a state of discord with nature and society.

When nature (or entailment) is not at fault, the bodily discordants are occasioned by intemperance, irregularity, excess beyond the powers of nature, ignorance of the animal economy, personal filthiness, and slothful habits. Those of the mind display themselves in malignant temper, in inordinate selfishness, in want of time to exert the charities of life toward others; and the consequences are self-reprobation, discontentedness, hypocrisy, meanness, hating, and being hated.

It is difficult to be truly happy and to say to ourselves that we are so, because all the virtues and exalted wisdom are necessary to the fruition of complete happiness, and a single vice or error alloys the whole. False estimates and incongruous expectations *mar* the happiness of many upon whom nature and society have conferred their apparent means of full enjoyment; while acute feelings, warmth of temper, and high prejudices and partialities deprive others of the urbanity of manners and equanimity of temper, which promote cheerfulness and reconcile man to man.

The mischievous error of the world in ignoring moral honesty, in assigning virtue to success, and crime to misfortune, improperly substitutes a heart-rending solicitude about the world's opinion, in place of the satisfaction of intending well, and having with integrity done our best. The envy of the unworthy, who think others more happy than they know themselves to be, begets slanders, backbiting, and malignant whispers;

and to surmount these, calls for a degree of patience and vigor of understanding not possessed by all.

Therefore, it appears obvious from the foregoing illustration that our happiness and misery are to a very great extent, placed in our own hands; that we are the *arbiters* of our own fate, and that—

THE WORLD IS WHAT WE MAKE IT.

"Oh! call not this a vale of tears,
   A world of gloom and sorrow;
One-half the grief that o'er us comes,
   From self we often borrow.
The earth is beautiful and good;
   How long will men mistake it?
The folly is within ourselves;
   The world is what we make it.

"Did we but strive to make the best
   Of troubles that befall us,
Instead of meeting cares half-way,
   They would not so appall us.
Earth has a spell for loving hearts;
   Why should we seek to break it?
Let's scatter flowers instead of thorns—
   The world is what we make it.

"If *truth* and *love* and *gentle words*
   We took the pains to nourish,
The seeds of discontent would die,
   And peace and comfort flourish.
Oh! has not each some kindly thought?
   Then let's at once awake it,
Believing that, for good or ill,
   The world is what we make it."

LOVE IS A BIRD OF SUMMER SKIES.

"There is a solace sweet and dear,
  Within this world of woe and fear—
It is when woman's soothing word
In sympathy with man's is heard.

"There is a joy most thrilling sweet,
  When lips with lips impassioned meet;
When man with woman's love is blessed,
And hearts to hearts are fondly pressed.

"Her lovely voice, that magic power,
  Can cheer the pilgrim's lonely hour;
So softly sweet its soothing lay,
Oh! it drives dull cares far away."

PART II.

AN ESSAY ON MAN,

UNDER FIFTEEN CAPTIONS.

CHAPTER I.

HIS MIND AND SENSES—RESULT OF ORGANIZATION.

"Know then thyself, presume not God to scan;
The greatest study of mankind is man."

It has been truly said that "the greatest study of mankind is man." Indeed, throughout all human society there is not furnished a theme so grand, so vastly important, nor yet any one so much neglected. For the reading public as a general thing take very little interest in any moral or philosophical subjects, particularly such as pertain to the great science of man—to the improvement of their own race. Hence the writer is well aware that he has undertaken an arduous and fruitless task, and might as well, perhaps, amuse himself by throwing pebbles at the moon.

Yes, the study of man is a very important subject, and to investigate it properly, we must take reason, experience, and common sense for our guide, otherwise we may be led astray by conflicting opinions, and thereby deceive ourselves and others.

When I consider the intellectual character of man, I am struck with the fact that his mind and body have an intimate and necessary connection; for whatever the mind may be, and in whatever way it is connected with its material dwelling-place, one thing seems to be certain—it does not display its powers until it has been acted upon by the senses.

This fact leads to the belief of the materiality of the mind, and has been the subject of many able, interesting, and instructive discussions.

It is clear that the physical and mental action of one human being is not known to any other only by and through the senses.

These truths force on us the necessity of considering the action of the senses in connection with, and inseparably from, what is known of the qualities of the mind.

The human mind has been the subject of many learned works. These have been given to the world at different periods. Each successive author has had the opportunity of studying the theories of his predecessors, and of adopting, modifying, disproving, or rejecting them, and of attempting to establish his own. I will not undertake to compare the different systems, if the ability to do so could be assumed, nor to say which of them should be received, nor which should be rejected; but it is obvious that all those written prior to the discovery of the *true laws of mind*, by Gaul and Spurshcim, must have been very imperfect, for how could men write correctly on mental science when measurably ignorant of the fundamental laws of *mind*, as set forth by the great science of phrenology.

It is merely proposed, as sufficient for the present object, to pass a few moments in the examination of intellectual acts as the simplest and easiest, and perhaps the most satisfactory mode of instruction.

No one knows how his earliest steps in the acquirement of knowledge were taken; but he knows what the fact is with his juniors, and he infers truly that his own course must have been similar. It is thus known to every one that in earliest infancy the human being is of all animals the most helpless; that months elapse before there is any apparent sensation but that which arises from the want of food or a sense of suffering. The eye and the ear are for a long time insensible, and when age enough is obtained to put their organs to use, they have everything apparently to learn. The discrimination between different sounds, and knowledge of figure, magnitude, color and distance of external objects, are very slowly obtained, and only then by experiments often repeated. Less is known of the acquirements of the other senses, excepting that the sense of feeling appears to be always on the alert, and its disagreeable effects are frequently manifested. After some few years, all the senses appear to have undergone the discipline of experience to the effect of answering the common purposes of life. What the senses have attained to by experience must depend, of course, on the sort of experience, or on the employment in which they have been engaged. The senses of a number of young persons who are equally gifted by nature in this respect will acquire different habits, according to the accidental circumstances in which they are placed. Children brought up in a city, those who have been only in a small village, those who have been regularly at school, and those who have been employed in agriculture, will have their senses very differently disciplined. If each of these were brought together, and acted upon at the same time by the same causes, each class would be differently affected, and the individuals of the same class would be affected in different degrees. The senses, therefore, may be said to be subjects of instruction by experience from early infancy. The only proposition which it is necessary to establish is, that the senses are subjects of discipline and of habit in every person, whatever his vocation in life may be. Another proposition which is self-evident is, that all knowledge of external objects and substances *must* be obtained through the senses. Those who are blind from birth can not have any knowledge of forms, of comparative distances, except the imperfect knowledge which the other senses give; and they must be entirely ignorant of color and of all other acquirements to which the use of the eye is indispensable. The deaf from birth must be entirely ignorant of all knowledge of sounds—the senses are therefore necessary avenues of knowledge to the mind.

It must be admitted, therefore, that the action of the senses is indispensable to the development of the mind; and from this well-known fact the materialists argue that the mind is not independent of itself, but the result of material organization. It is solely through the operation of physical machinery that mental effects are brought about; for each act of the mind requires for its production the resolution of a portion of the material brain. Where there is no brain, there is no manifestation of mind; though we often hear the remark made that mind is something entirely independent of organization. But we might as well say that music is independent of the instrument, or that we can have the fragrance of the rose without the rose itself. Nothing seems plainer to me than that mind is the result of organization, for without the latter there are no senses by which knowledge is communicated to the mind.

There is no intelligence where there is no sense, and no sense where there are no organs of sense.

The mind is in a good or bad condition according as the brain is healthy or diseased, and now if mind does not depend on organization, why should the derangement of the latter have such an effect on the former as we often witness? Why should a blow on the head dethrone the reason for a longer or shorter time, if the mind be independent of the body? We ought not to see this result, and certainly should not, if the mind were a distinct entity, separate and apart from the organization. In that case, it would no more be affected by a material agency, or wound, than Mr. Brady would be injured bodily by a blow given Mr. Tracy.

But this is not the fact, for one mind can not be injured by what may happen to another, and we have yet to see the mind and body united where the derangement of the latter did not affect the former.

Until the pretended philosophers can produce a case to the contrary, they do not, as it appears to me, make much progress in proving the existence of mind independent of the body. When the brain is distempered, or malformed, the mind is seriously impaired or idiotic. Did any one ever know of a diseased brain and a healthy mind in the same person? This intimate connection and dependence between the mind and body, necessarily subjects both to one law. This is in accordance with the economy displayed everywhere in nature; for no new element is ever introduced to perform a function which can be accomplished by the extension or further development of an existing agent.

But a great many intelligent men suppose that the mind is a perfect independent being, and that it is so from the commencement of life. They seem to think that it is not inconsistent with some analogies in nature; that the mind or soul is originally given to every human being, and that the action of life developes and makes it whatever it becomes. But it is more reasonable, I think, to suppose that the mind expands, and is progressive in conformity to the action made on it first through the senses, and then by its own operation.

CHAPTER II.

HIS NATURE IS EVER THE SAME.

TURN to the "proverbs" of the most ancient nations and to their moral laws; to the Hindu Vedas, to the Mosaic code, the Persian Shaster, the codes of Menu and Confucius, the Proverbs of Solomon, and those of nations two thousand years before his time; read ours to-day, and those of any extant people, and tell me if they are not still the same—if man's character to-day here, and everywhere, is not a perfect impression from those stereotyped plates representing his moral features in all past ages?

Point out a single crime in their catalogues that has been redeemed from the list, or one that can not be shown in Christian statutes to-day? Read the histories, the poems, and the ancient plays of Persia, Hindostan, and all other countries, and you will find that exactly the same round of characters formed every social group as now, with the same passions and propensities; that crimes and human infirmities existed in the same proportion as now.

After all the educating, lecturing, and preaching that has been done to change man, here he is pretty much as these early records paint him—the same complaining, faithless, quarreling, selfish, jealous, bigoted *infidel* that he was then—proving conclusively that the same physical circumstances have and ever will produce the same moral effects by an inflexible law. There never has been—there is not now—on earth a society sufficiently large that is not composed of the same round of characters, of good and evil intermixed in the same relative proportions—the rich and the poor, the virtuous and the frail, the fanatic and the hypocrite, the flirt and the gossip, the thrifty and the unthrifty, fast boys, loafing husbands, thefts, riots, suicides, brawls, murders, burglaries, etc. There never was a man who did not revolve, with some obliquity of the axis, around some ruling passion. The rose has always had its thorns, the diamond its specks, and the best man his failings; and the records of all countries confirm our observation, that every variety of legal offense bears a constant ratio to the number of inhabitants in the same places.

Now if this order of things has always existed, or for thousands of years, under every form of religion and government, who can resist the conviction of its *necessity* and its immutability?

Seeing, then, that man's character is persistent, and that the current of events that leads to marked epochs is the same among all people, how easy is the art of prophecy! Only leave your dates blank or ambiguous, and you can scarcely prophesy a possible event that will not be sure of fulfillment some time or other, especially if any one is interested in making out its accomplishment.

Yes, man has ever been in all ages, in every country, and under every form of government and religion, a faithless, selfish, bigoted, and persecuting infidel or hypocrite; but such character did not proceed from his primitive or God-given nature, because his mental, moral, and religious-attributes are capable, under proper discipline, of a high state of civilization and refinement, much higher than has ever yet been attained.

Indeed, the time will surely come when our race will be elevated as far above what it now is as we are above the most ignorant and rude savages; when strife, persecutions, murders, and wars will almost entirely cease, and when peace, friendship, and love will greatly abound. We are faithless, selfish, and deceitful hypocrites merely because we have been for untold ages taught to be such—because we are ignorant of ourselves and of our race; not knowing the kind of beings with whom we had to deal; ignorant of the laws which controlled our own minds, and consequently our affections and actions.

Nor could anything better have been reasonably expected, since our teachers, preachers, and legislators have ever been (and are now) so ignorant of natural laws, of themselves, and of their pupils, auditors, and constituents. So ignorant now, that just before and during the late rebellion, our highly educated and *honest* but ignorant ministers did, by their silly partisan and unholy preaching, demoralize or completely destroy thousands of well-doing and respectable churches. Hence such "order of things" was a natural necessity or result of ignorance—a "necessity" only as a promotive or incentive to improvement, to progress. Then—

> Why blame the thistles for having grown,
> After we ourselves the seeds had sown.

CHAPTER III.

HIS POSITIVE AND SELF-KNOWLEDGE.

Nothing but positive knowledge obtained through the medium of the five physical senses, and supported by tangible evidences found inside the regular order of nature, should ever be taught to the young and rising generations; for the inculcating of mere opinions is burdening the next age with the errors, superstitions, and delusions of the present, and impedes much the progress of intellect. We should teach the youth in our schools every kind of useful knowledge, all the primary and higher branches of a useful English education, and postpone all preparations for future life to their proper time, proper places, and preceptors; and leave the application of the same until future conditions and circumstances shall dictate the convenience and necessity of acting or forming opinions. By this time their minds will be pretty well matured, their investigating and discriminating faculties developed, enabling them thereby to analyze and compare ideas, and finally to select more properly such professions, trades, etc., as may best suit their peculiar tastes, conditions, and constitutional adaptations. Advising, influencing, and, as is too often the case, indirectly coercing persons, young and old, how to think and act in such and such circumstances, is only declaring what you think is best for them in their situation, and is therefore liable to mislead and ultimately to produce more harm than good. The safest way, when asked for advice, is to give all the *positive* knowledge you possess on the subject, then leave the individual to judge as best he can.

Opinions are so various, contradictory, and changeable, depending on incidents, temper, constitution, and situation, many of them beyond our control, that they ought not to be the subject of dispute and persecution, so common among professing people, much less impressed on the plastic minds of our children during their education.

And another thing which very much retards the progress of positive knowledge, is the quality of books and other reading matter thrown broadcast over our general country, the three-fourths of which is mere rubbish, sophistry, trash, tales, fiction, etc., only calculated to incumber, debilitate, and demoralize the minds of our youth. But this is a fast age, and people must think and act only as they have been taught—only according to the styles and fashions of the day—anything and everything, right or wrong, for popularity, patronage, etc. No time this for changing opinions, for looking after *moral duties*, positive knowledge, etc.

Yet the change of opinion ought to be proof of more accurate information; but as it is a confession of being formerly in the wrong, our false self-esteem is opposed to avowing it, and ignorant people attach some weakness and disgrace to those who change their mode of thinking on any subjects.

Indeed, nothing is more changeable or precarious than opinions; for one who obtains possession of power has not the same opinions as when he was subject to obey power.

One who obtains riches does not hold the same opinions as when he was poor. When a man is sick he thinks differently from what he did when in good health. A weak man thinks differently from a strong man; a young man from an old man; a wise man from an unwise man, and any and every man who acquires more correct information must change his opinions. Change circumstances and you change interest, and as certainly change opinions. One may as reasonably quarrel with another for not using the same kinds of food, for having hair of a different color, a nose longer or shorter, *as for having an opinion different from his own.* Yet the arbitrary assumption that all ought to think with the strongest party, is the origin of all intolerance and persecution.

Again, many intelligent but deluded men run their opinions to great excess, opposing religion as not only useless, but injurious to society, such as Voltaire, Payne, etc. But I am constrained to differ very much with all such extreme men, from the fact that no person ever yet heard of the existence of civilized society in the absence of Bibles and gospel preaching. Indeed, without the churches, universal discord and anarchy would soon overrun the whole country; and the great excess of church influence will as surely bring about, sooner or later, the same ruinous results, as the early ages have proven to a demonstration. Hence it is obvious that it is not religion which creates the trouble, but the abuse of it.

As there are opposing forces and warring elements throughout all nature, so there are and needs to be in society, and everything in nature, morals, and religion tends to the great and universal law of equilibrium. Therefore, we always need in society a proper proportion of church people and non-conformists (or outsiders); the one class being as necessary as the other; the one the life and salvation of the other, for just remove all the outsiders, and soon there will be no insiders; and just abolish either of the two great political parties, and very soon infolerance and despotism will reign supreme. The one is a necessary check on the other.

For those who oppose us in politics, in religion, or upon any other subjects, are, in the end, our best friends and benefactors—*they are our sentinels on the watch-tower while we sleep, and vice versa;* for the world exists but by conflict, and is only maintained by opposition; we ever find one force pitted against another, and all things find their contrarieties to be the foundation of their preservation and their perpetuity.

Then what are the churches, the outsiders, and the political parties eternally wrangling and quarreling about?

They are quarreling simply because they do n't know any better; because they know so very little of themselves—of the great laws of mind; because they are not sufficiently enlightened and refined; because they believe that the mind acts voluntary, and hence that people can believe just what they choose in despite of their past education and surroundings; because they know so little of the moral duties and relations existing between man and man, between man and society, and between man and his Creator; because they lack positive knowledge which would teach them better than to annoy and slander their neighbors merely because they are obliged to differ with them in opinion. And without this practical and positive knowledge, which few possess, *it is impossible for any of us to be uniform and practical moral or religious men and women;* yet all such knowledge is carefully kept out of the schools, out of the churches, and out of all books except such as are written upon phrenological principles. Indeed, the masses of the people seemed determined not to learn anything of the great science of mind—*determined not. to learn those natural laws and principles which underlie and control all their actions.*

People can be quite *honest,* yet fault-finding, persecuting, selfish, and *mean* in a thousand ways, as every day's experience proves most conclusively; all for the want of a little education in the right direction, an education in first principles, in men, and in such things, duties, and relations as pertain to practical life—all on account of their possessing only a superficial and restricted education as above indicated, and their consequent self-inflation, unkindness, and presumption. But as a very general thing, what they lack in wisdom is bountifully made up to them in self-conceit; hence feeling secure and self-sufficient, never learn until too late, that a

> "Little learning is a dangerous thing,
> Drink deep, or taste not the Pierian spring;
> For shallow draughts intoxicate the brain,
> But drinking deep will sober us again."

To illustrate. The ancient Catholics persecuted the Protestants, even unto death, by fire and the sword, merely for opinion's sake, for only imaginary wrongs.

In the fifteenth, sixteenth, and seventeenth centuries, the Christians of England, Scotland, France, Germany, and North America tried, condemned, and executed by fire and the sword, in all, perhaps, half a million of unfortunate and innocent mortals, merely for witchcraft. And the Christians of the New England States persecuted and tortured, in a cruel manner, the peaceable "Quakers," only for a difference of opinion.

All this savage cruelty was inflicted merely for opinion's sake—for wrongs which existed only in their ignorant imaginations; because there is no doubt but they were all as honest and well meaning as the best of us are at this time, and considered themselves not only *moral* but *religious* men.

Yet everybody will now admit that they were practically not only *immoral*, but extremely *wicked*.

But many honest people will palliate those ancient outrages by averring that they were done in the dark ages—in the dark ages I must admit; and this is rather a dusky age, as the sequel will show. Indeed, but for a few noble minds, comparatively speaking, and the efficiency of our civil laws, very soon would the dark clouds hover around our horizon—soon would our sun, too, be eclipsed—soon would scenes of persecution and torture take place, such as would astonish the world; for the same ignorance, prejudice, and vindictiveness prevails at this time to a great degree. For example: The political parties all over the United States are ready, now and then, to almost destroy each other; and have not thousands of honest and good men in the Southern States been recently shot down and starved to death in cool blood, merely because they *honestly* differed in opinion with the opposite party? And why do we, who boast so much of our moral and religious training—we, the modern Puritans of the Northern States—give our influence, money, and votes to create state laws by which houses—sinks of iniquity—are chartered, and ignorant demons licensed to deal out their liquid and soul-destroying poisons—licensed to rob, starve, and disgrace the mothers and their helpless children—to debase and to *derange* the husbands and fathers that they may ultimately rob and slay their fellow-men? And what next? Our intelligent courts go to work coolly, deliberately, and religiously, and incarcerate them in the abodes of misery and degradation, which disgrace and ruin them, *their innocent and amiable wives and children forever; they go to work and commit upon them legalized moral murder—legalized murder.*

For all this mischief the *ignorant* but *honest* voters are responsible. But I would not have my readers believe that I am opposed to chastisement for felons and assassins, etc. No, indeed; we should always have houses of correction and reformation for such evil-doers; organized and conducted in a manner similar to our state prisons, but bearing a different name, and quite a different character, and where such persons could be properly educated, reclaimed, and finally returned to society; while all such as could not be so reclaimed and safely set at liberty should be confined during life at labor, but not abused.

Now this does not gingle like legal, moral, or physical murder, but like humanity and true christianity.

Are not the churches eternally persecuting each other and all "outsiders," particularly the Materialists, Universalists, and Spiritualists, and *vice versa?* This they do *not through any ill-design* or *natural meanness*, but solely on account of their ignorance of moral and mental science.

Again, it is known that before and during the late rebellion, political excitement was very great, and that, in consequence, thousands of prosperous and respectable churches were either entirely broken up or badly demoralized—the work, mostly, of Republican preachers, who, by their *silly* and *uncharitable* language, drove out, in many instances, nearly all the Democratic element, and *vice versa*. Now the great majority of these ministers were *honest* and *well-meaning and highly educated men*, but were, notwithstanding, very ignorant of human nature—ignorant of those natural laws which control and govern the actions and affections of men.

And again, for more than two centuries, nearly the

whole people of the United States had been by their suffrages and money propagating the institution of slavery, which, notwithstanding it aided very much in the early development of the resources of a new and fertile country which had been but recently discovered, peopled and made opulent the barren hills of New England, and opened up the rich and miasmatic regions of the South, is, after all, an institution incompatible with true moral and religious principles and good government—demoralizing and revolutionary in its results; and only for the *ignorance*, depravity, and cupidity of our people, both North and South, would have been peaceably abolished fifty or sixty years ago. But perhaps its work was not then finished—*the day of retribution had to come*, the people needed education and progression; and it seems that customs and institutions never give place only when, and after their missions are accomplished, they yield to the supreme law which determines their *utility* and their *limits*. Before that fatal period is reached, no opposition can be effectual. No conspiracy, no revolt, no violence, can overthrow a custom or an institution before the time has come for its dissolution. It is maintained by an eternal fiat—by an irresistible force against which all human efforts are of no avail.

"During the whole of these proceedings, as above written, the ancient clergy, both Catholic and Protestant, were in possession of revelation as fully and freely as they are to day. And in Scotalnd, in particular, the reformation had been completed, and the people put in possession of the Bible for nearly a century before the cessation of these prosecutions and executions for witchcraft."

And North America has always been blessed with the Bible, and with all other lights and advantages necessary to enlighten, moralize, and refine its inhabitants far above all this low slang and persecution merely for a difference of opinion, without any regard whatever to the moral acts and merits of the individuals—merely because we all can not see through the same glasses—merely for wrongs such as witchcraft, unbelief in this creed or in that, for riding through the air on a broomstick, etc., etc. ("In England, thirty thousand were put to death for the last offense"—*by little Solomons,* of whom *we have to-day legions**). Now all the above-named foolishness, troubles, persecutions, and executions were inflicted merely for the want of a proper degree of *self-knowledge*, which will keep a man calm and equal in his temper, and wise and cautious in his conduct. It will enable him to make the proper allowance for the opinions and acts of his fellow-men; to learn his own ignorance and unworthiness, and hence to place a higher estimate on all men; to enjoy life happily, and thereby avoid many vexations and troubles.

In short, most of the misfortunes which men meet with may be traced up to and resolved into self-ignorance. Indeed, ignorance is the great and unpardonable sin—the primitive cause of nine-tenths of all the troubles and misfortunes which overtake our race. We

---

*Parrington's History.

may complain of nature, of bad luck, and of men; but the fault, if we carefully examine it, will generally be found to be our own. Our rashness and imprudence, which arises from self-ignorance, either brings our troubles on us or increases them. Want of a mind properly enlightened and refined will make any affliction double; but it is next thing to impossible to fasten any affliction on a mind well versed in moral science, on a mind truly *philosophically enlightened*, on a mind capable of extracting good, *present or future*, from all circumstances. What a long train of difficulties do sometimes proceed from only *one* wrong step in our conduct into which our self-ignorance betrayed us; and all the lectures and sermons delivered from the schools and pulpits in condemnation of vice and crime, ambition, vanity, and folly, will avail as little as reproof to the tempest, while laws, habits, example, and education draw mankind into the vortex of luxury, dissipation, dishonesty, falsehood, superstition, and contention.

Were mankind but more generally convinced of the importance and necessity of such self-knowledge, and possessed with a due regard for it; did they but know the true way to attain it; and under a proper sense of its excellence, and the fatal effects of self-ignorance, did they but make it their business every day to cultivate it, how soon should we find a happy alteration in the manners and dispositions of men. But the mischief of it is, *men will not think for themselves;* they had much sooner other men think for them—sooner believe this sophistry or that, merely because other men believed it.

But if the great object of social life were to exhibit good sense and correct conduct as the *only* true criterion of human excellence—if this truth were generally understood and acted upon—riches, power, and empty fashion would soon lose much of their influence; and men, pursuing nothing but intellectual improvement in the skillful use of their undestanding, would advance in true science, and consequently in well-doing—would live to a good age, and answer the ends and purposes for which they were created.

CHAPTER IV.

HIS EDUCATION.

'Tis education that forms the common mind,
Just as the twig is bent the tree's inclined.

WHAT is man without education? Then as he is a gregarious, moral, social, and religious being, and *must* live in society, he should be educated. His intellectual, moral, and social faculties should be well developed, particularly as his greatest enjoyments are derived from the exercise of the moral and social laws.

How happy they render him when all else is gone, and how miserable would he not be, with all'the wealth of the world, if denied their rich blessings. Therefore, the first object of every family and community should be to teach its members the great and all-important lesson, "to know thyself," to know the physical, moral, and social laws which must ever govern them in all they *are* or ever can be, and which must necessarily shape and determine their future destiny, not only as individuals but as nations—to know the moral and social *duties* and *relations* existing between man and man, man and society, between man and his Creator; then, and not until then, will they ever know their neighbors, how to treat them, and how to sympathize with them; and not until then will they ever cease their extreme proscriptions and persecutions merely for opinion's sake. But what are we now doing in that direction? Next thing to nothing. Yet our general country is inundated with respectable journals which devote their columns to almost all subjects, particularly to politics, religion, agriculture, improvement of stock, etc. But scarcely once in seven years do we find an article on the all-important subject of man. Poor man, he is not worth looking after! Nothing is said about the elevation of his own race, although, as Doctor Combe says, "we take great pains to improve our horses, cattle, sheep, and swine; yea, even our dogs, but never once think of the improvement of our own race." And nothing is said about the causes of his present physical and mental imbecility and consequent mortality, which is so destructive and alarming, sweeping off, by premature death, multiplied millions, and also filling our poor-houses and asylums with other millions of debilitated, deaf, blind, and idiotic mortals, all the legitimate work of neglected and outraged laws.

Then what means should be employed, what more shall we teach to remedy this great failure, to improve the condition of the masses, that general intelligence, self-reliance, self-respect, liberality, peace and happiness might *more* greatly abound; that we may lay the ax at the root of the tree; that we may build our moral and social edifice on a solid rock, and that we may finally learn that great lesson, to know ourselves, and hence to know and to love all mankind.

We should teach in our families, in our schools and upon all occasions, first principles, the universal and fundamental laws of our being, and of the external world, the imperative duty and necessity of thinking for ourselves upon all subjects. The necessity and capacity of reasoning from causes to their effects, of analizing and comparing ideas, thereby separating truth from sophistry, and of never allowing ourselves to believe any theory, doctrine, or circumstance, until after we have found, inside the pale of nature, some tangible reasons deduced from common sense, experience and sound philosophy.

We should also teach in our families, in our schools, and upon all possible occasions, the great science of physiology in all its bearings, the laws of phrenology, of marriage, of entailments, and of the temperaments, upon which depends, more than upon all other means, the future elevation and salvation of our race. For if the crude material, the physical and mental man, be not right, the hand of the polisher can never turn out a good article; no, not any more than we can make a "Sampson" out of an ordinary man; not any more than we can make a skillful mechanic out of a boy not naturally adapted to that business, or a temperate, candid, and honest man out of a boy largely developed for intemperance, deception, and dishonesty; not any more than we can make a lamb out of a young lion; notwithstanding education has a powerful influence in shaping the character of men.

And without this knowledge, we can never know but very little of the all-important science of man, his capacity and peculiarities, of his effeminacy, degeneracy, and consequent depravity and mortality. Indeed, it is well demonstrated, and now an admitted fact among the learned physiologists, that a great part of our crime and imbecility, and consequent mortality, is produced, directly or indirectly, from our illegal marriages—by alliances not constitutionally adapted, and which never fail to afflict the unfortunate offspring with debility, disease, and premature death.

We should not only educate the *mind*, but the fingers, hands, and body—the whole man; for the body is the instrument upon which the mind plays the tune of life; and if we desire music harmonious and sweet, we must have a good instrument and keep it in prime order—alive in every nerve, sound in every limb, and perfect in every part; yes, to make the *education* of our children worth much, it should be well mixed with physical exercise, with useful labor performed in the fields, in the garden, kitchen, and parlor. They should go to school awhile, then labor awhile; they should toil and perspire outdoors and indoors, whenever labor is needed; live on plain food, drink cold water, and abhor whisky and tobacco.

They should let the glorious sun shine on them, the refreshing winds blow on them, let it rain and freeze on them, etc. This is the way, the only way, to make *men* and *women*, to build up good physical and mental constitutions, to develop the whole man, to prolong life, and to have it useful to themselves and to their country.

But education as now given to our children, particularly in towns and cities, is almost useless, a waste of money and humanity; for thousands and millions of them are kept in the schools from seven until they are twenty-one years old, without being required to soil their hands by any useful labor; growing up in effeminacy (soon to fall) like so many butter-weeds.

In the meantime, vast numbers of them contract ruinous habits of idleness and extravagance, and finally leave school with only a partial book education, acquired at the expense of health and morals; consequently they are ever after too feeble or too idle and extravagant to make their educations, though ever complete, available.

And strange to tell, those baneful results are chiefly produced from the foolish and reckless manner in which our schools, high and low, are conducted; the educators, great and small, compelling their pupils to waste more than the one-half of every term in memorizing and declaiming nonsense, writing and reciting essays, preparing for exhibitions, etc., none of which (though necessary) should ever be allowed to interrupt a school except at the end of a five or six months' term.

And also requiring their scholars to carry along at the same time *three* and four studies; than which a more simple and injurious practice could not be adopted, because one study forever interferes with another, from the fact it is as impossible for any mind to concentrate on more than one study at a time, as it is for a sun-glass to converge the rays of the sun on two or more points at one and the same time.

And any school-boy ought to have sense enough to know that without steady application and concentration, it is impossible to make much progress in any science, or even in ordinary business. (But it must not be understood that I would have scholars closely confined to abstract studies from morn till noon, and from noon till night; but their minds should be, when necessary, relieved by lessons in reading, penmanship, etc.)

The writer well recollects when this practice was introduced by Eastern men into the vicinity of Cincinnati (about the year 1825), and it was then called a "Yankee trick" to swindle the people. It is yet (with the rest) but a "Yankee trick," an intolerable outrage on every community.

Then what can be the reason that so many of our pious, respectable, and well-educated professors and teachers, not only tolerate, but participate in practices or methods of teaching so repugnant to common sense and all human experience?

Is it because they are after all really ignorant? No, that *can not* be the case. Then there must be some other cause; then there may be some large pecuniary interest at the bottom of all this mischief—some great organized league gotten up (long since) for the ostensible purpose of prolonging the pupilage of our children to ten and twelve years, so as to make their business sufficiently remunerative to maintain our present armies of pedagogues, and for other purposes and interests no less nefarious.

Then, fathers and philanthropists, why not dispense with those hot-beds of idleness, vanity, and effeminacy, and go to work without delay for your children and for your race?

Go to work before it is too late, and snatch the coming generations from almost total ruin; reconstruct your common and graded schools in a sensible and judicious manner, organize manual labor colleges, and thereby obviate those demoralizing and destructive consequences.

And more especially, fathers, as the mental organizations of a large majority of your children are such that much book-learning, with the consequent idleness and extravagance, will be ruinous to them, from the fact they will become debilitated, paralyzed, and demoralized; hence their domestic and financial attributes will become very much impaired, thereby rendering them measurably useless to themselves and to their country—only fit to crowd the sideways and churches; to annoy and swindle the laboring class; to *waste* what they may inherit; and, lastly, to *afflict* society with an offspring far inferior to themselves.

But if you *really* love your children, and wish to promote their *true* and *best* interest, give them all, if possible, a good and practical common-school education, well mixed with physical labor, which will qualify them for almost any business in society.

Now, if any one, two, or more of them should naturally "thirst and hunger" for greater proficiency in the sciences—should aspire for any of the professions—then assist them cautiously, a little now and a little then.

Throw them mostly on their own resources, not neglecting to administer occasionally the elixir of life (domestic labor). Cultivate them to self-reliance—to *self-reliance*. Yes, compel them ultimately to save themselves, which they will *surely* do if there be in them much emulation and energy; but if there be not it will be useless to *waste* much money on them. Then put them to work; put them to some honorable and useful labor, and no doubt they will make worthy and respectable citizens; will fill their mission here on earth; will live out their three-score and ten years; will glide down the gentle stream of life to its terminus, the world the better by their having lived in it.

> "A little learning is a dangerous thing,
> Drink deep, or taste not the Pierian spring;
> For shallow draughts intoxicate the brain,
> But drinking deep will sober it again."

All the above-named laws, sciences, principles, and relations are naturally connected together, and should be taught in all graded and higher schools to the exclusion, as a general rule, of the dead languages and of the other branches of minor importance, which only protract the pupilage of our children, and, in the end, compel them to remain ignorant of many of the most useful sciences so *very necessary* in after life.

But is it not a humiliating and disgraceful fact, that many of the above-mentioned laws and sciences, as *necessary as life itself*, are not only ignored, but scoffed at in many of our best schools, and by multiplied thousands of the *so-called learned ones*, very many of whom not only claim the right to lead, but even to shape the public mind.

All such are far behind the present age, and are doomed to share the fate of those who persecuted such immortal benefactors as Columbus, Harvey, Fulton, and the Tuscan astronomer, Galileo, who, in his seventieth year, was forced by the unholy inquisition to retract his theory under the penalities of death.

But it was even then too late, for the divine thought had reached the boundless wires of heaven.

Just so it is with the inspired thoughts of Drs. Gall, Spursheim, Combe, and others. It is too late, and nothing can stop them until all scoffers are silenced—until they shall circumscribe the whole earth, carry convictions to all nations, to every school, and to every family.

A man can not be a Christian unless he be strictly moral; to be moral, he must live in obedience to the laws of his being and of society; to live in obedience to these laws, he must first know them—must understand those relations, principles, and influences which underlie and control all his actions and affections—must know himself.

CHAPTER V.

HIS MORAL ACCOUNTABILITY.

This is a very interesting subject, and one on which there are various and conflicting opinions; but it will be admitted by every one that man is by his physical and intellectual qualities very much distinguished from all other animals, and that he is much more so by those which we call the moral. He is perhaps the only animal who is capable of knowing beforehand whether an intended act will or will not conform to some known law or rule of right. It is equally certain that he only, of all animals, is capable of forming correct and systematic rules of action and of conforming his conduct to the same. And notwithstanding the physical, mental, and moral nature of man may be somewhat mysterious, the powers and attributes which he possesses are amply sufficient, when properly cultivated, to dispel all doubts concerning his duties, relations, and obligations as a citizen.

I will not attempt to settle a question much discussed among moral philosophers, whether man has or has not that natural perception of right and wrong which is called the moral sense; but he is certainly placed here in a very different relation to nature from all other animals—that he only has the capacity to improve his condition, and to ascend from a state of infancy—to progress onward and upward as to his intellectual and moral qualities to a high state of superiority.

And it is now well demonstrated that this capability is controlled and directed by fixed and immutable laws; that among them is the necessity of being able to discern what will advance his happiness, and also what will retard it, or produce disorder and suffering. Whether the cultivation of his faculties does or does not develop and bring into action the moral sense, in like manner as the cultivation of his faculties brings into action other powers of his mind, as I know it does, is an open question.

It may be admitted that the rude and uncultivated mind of man is not furnished with rules of right and wrong, so as to be capable of discerning between virtue and vice, or anything which is itself good or bad, unless it be in a very limited degree. I suppose it to be true, however, that man has not been known anywhere entirely destitute of all perception of right and wrong, though he has been found in many parts of the earth with very rude and imperfect perceptions of such knowledge.

I entertain no doubt that what may be called the moral sense does exist in the mind as a faculty, in all men to some extent, as a necessary consequence of their existence as men; and this sense may be developed and disciplined in like manner as the other faculties of the mind may be; and that by suitable cultivation this moral sense acquires a discriminating power, which may be called almost intuitive with respect to right and wrong. Indeed, it seems reasonable to suppose that there are very many persons who have this sense so developed by long-continued discipline, that they judge almost infallibly, as soon as a proposition is presented to them, of its character in relation to the most refined rules of fitness and propriety.

If I am right in this supposition, I think the moral sense is derived from a clear perception and a ready application of the laws which nature has prescribed for human conduct, and from like perception and application of the conventional laws which originate in social life. In proportion as the mind becomes well instructed in the meaning and use of the former description of laws, those which are of human institution are found to be right or wrong, just as they do or do not conform to those laws. I can not resist the conviction that if man is to be happy, he must be so by conforming to laws which nature has prescribed; and this purpose would evidently be defeated if those who are the objects of laws were not capable of comprehending them, and of making their own laws consistent with them.

In a multitude of instances the duty of obedience to laws, whether taken to be natural or human, must depend upon an immediate perception of their application to that which is to be done or to be avoided. To this it may be answered, that this is no more than the use of that intelligence which discipline imparts to all the intellectual faculties.

Consequently, it would seem that if a man was born with feeble mental and moral faculties, and surrounded by circumstances which forbade his cultivating them, he should not be held so accountable as others who were more favored—as others more intellectual and discriminating; for it is admitted by all that the idiot is not accountable at all to the moral or social laws—he is alone amenable to the organic and physical—he will, by a slip of the foot, fall as hard and get hurt as much as a philosopher. Therefore, it is clear that the God of nature makes no allowance for ignorance or debility.

And now, in conclusion, allow me to state that whether there be such "moral sense" or not in the original formation of man, it will sufficiently answer all practical purposes to establish such moral sense by a proper course of training, by which he may attain to a knowledge of those laws and rules that are adapted to secure to him all the intelligence and happiness of which he is capable or should reasonably expect.

CHAPTER VI.

HIS PERSONAL FREEDOM.

THERE is nothing more certain than that every individual who lives on this terrestrial sphere came into it with a natural organization differing from that of every other *individual*. This, in the order of nature, fits him for the performance of a peculiar mission, and for particular duties, as is plainly shown by the great science of phrenology.

Now if this natural organization is in any way restrained, or the aspirations of the individual too much curbed, society may, perhaps, secure an outward compliance with what is termed custom and law. But where the mere dictates of expediency establish custom and law for society, they oppose the proper development of the individual, and consequently hinder the progress of society. I do not mean by these remarks that a proper restraint should not be exercised to prevent the commission of acts which militate against the welfare and peace of society. But while the rights of others are unmolested, the greatest freedom consistent with the public good should be allowed to every person, and none but shallow-pated bigots or constitutional tyrants will refuse such freedom to any one.

No ridiculous or petty restrictions should ever hamper

his natural tastes and inclinations. What one may enjoy and greatly approve, another may take no delight in, but severely censure.

The question may be merely a matter of opinion, and in the judgment of one good may result, and in the judgment of the other positive harm may ensue. Each will be sincere, and will be equally well supported by the opinions of others; but as far as a mere question of opinion is concerned, no one person or set of persons has the right to condemn another; for the largest liberty of opinion and of action should be guaranteed to all, and neither in the family circle, nor in the social walks of life, should any one seek to enforce his peculiar notions and tastes upon others.

The force of example and the general power of persuasion can accomplish far more than can ever be effected by arbitrary and despotic compulsion.

There are some communities which set up for themselves a certain standard of morals, or rather prejudices, and vainly bask in the sunshine of a belief, which to other men seem absurd and ridiculous. The time comes when an individual desires to settle among them, and he is expected to conform to all their customs and peculiarities; but if he resist, and express by his conduct his desire to follow his own notions, and that without in the least interfering with the rights of others, he immediately becomes the recipient of much low slang and persecution. He may be a moral, industrious, and useful citizen, yet all this amounts to nothing unless he has ample means and belongs to some of the popular and fashionable societies.

He is willing to move along quietly and mind his own business, but this trait of character many of his more self-pious neighbors seem to be almost entirely destitute of. People ought to attend to their own business more carefully and allow their neighbors to take care of theirs. They lose sight of the fact that a community *must* be just, liberal, and truly religious, not only in *words* and *pretentions*, but in their moral conduct, before it can set itself up as a fair model for all men to follow. They forget that every man has a right to do just as he pleases, so long as he sacredly regards the rights of others.

Too many of us are slaves of perverted habit; slaves of custom and fashion; slaves of an unenlightened public opinion, which is ready to crush the smallest exercise of the sovereignty of the individual; slaves of systems and laws which the world has outgrown, and which are but fetters to hinder our progress. Let all allow the same freedom to others, in thought and action, which they claim for themselves, and one great step will be taken in the progress of the world which society has long been waiting for, and which was never more needed than it is at present.

CHAPTER VII.

HIS SELF-IMPROVEMENT.

SELF-IMPROVEMENT consists in the growth of the mental organs and faculties; for the mind, in its voluntary capacity, is what makes the man. The mind is constituted to act voluntarily, and these voluntary acts, whether agreeable or disagreeable to the eyes of others, determine the character of the individual, but which, in reality, signify the character of the mind. There are two classes of minds—one conservative, the other progressive—and why? Because different minds have different degrees of cerebral growth and expansion. Conservative minds are apparently stationary, by growing or expanding so slowly that their field of mental vision or comprehension does not apparently widen or advance in the distance. Hence, their views become fixed or definite; whereas, if they possessed a more expansive comprehension, their field of thought would so widen, deepen, and lengthen that they would no longer be conservative, but progressive. The brain is the organ of the mind—the seat and source of all the passions and affections—and not the heart, as so many erroneously suppose; as well talk about the liver having high moral or immoral functions. It is true the heart frequently acts in sympathy with the mind—responds to it; but invariably the effect is first produced on the mind, and the various consequences follow—such as joy, grief, fear, anger, etc.—and which sometimes result in sudden deaths. Yea, the brain is a true representative of its perceptive, reflective, and potential character. Hence, its size, texture, and activity combined, bespeak the constitution of its indwelling mental power and principle; consequently, in proportion as the mind becomes more and more comprehensive, the quality or texture of the brain becomes correspondingly modified by being improved and elevated, and *vice versa*. Hence, mental improvement becomes, in reality, cerebral improvement, mental growth, or expansion; also, cerebral growth or expansion.

Consequently, the growth of the mental and phrenological organs is an actual index of a progressive mind; and whenever such growth is not present, it is equally an index of a conservative mind. On this principle is established the progressive and improving tendencies of children. Their brains, subject to the organic powers of their minds, gradually increase in size, and hence their field of mental vision proportionally widens, deepens, and lengthens, causing thereby new ideas or thoughts to unfold themselves to their comprehension. But when the day of full maturity overtakes them, then it is that they settle down on preconceived ideas or convictions as real conservatives. They are capable of seeing a certain distance, and being incapable of extending further, must stop—why? Because the proper incentive to a higher degree of mental action is wanting. Hence, they forever after merely float along, embracing the popular fashions, doctrines, and prejudices of the day; and at forty are less capable of reasoning from causes to effects than they were when only twenty years old.

Now, as an illustration of the foregoing, take the organs of order, ideality, and approbativeness. Their mental functions prompt their possessor to love the orderly and neat in everything. But if these organs be not well developed, their possessors will have no great dislike to disorder and confusion—to filth and grossness. All such citizens of towns and cities can, with great indifference, allow their dwelling-houses and all out-buildings to remain in a rough, unpainted, and dilapidated condition; their door-yards poorly fenced, and covered with trash and weeds; gates broken or dragging; the cows and pigs occasionally around the house, forbidding all flowers and shrubbery. And as a general thing in the towns, the stabling and surroundings are in a rough and disorderly fix—the gates dragging, the poor cows standing out in the chilling storms, the pigs shut up in their sties above their knees in cold mud or without bedding.

Yet these same men appear in their respective churches richly or duly and neatly fixed up, as if all things were right and comfortable at home. Now there are a great many citizens in Thorntown, Lebanon, and other places, who have never, perhaps, taken much notice of these things; I would therefore respectfully invite all such to take an evening walk, now and then, through their respective towns, and be cautioned.

And the farmers, as a class, are not a whit behind the inhabitants of the towns as regards their uncomely appearance at home; indeed, they are generally worse. All fencing around their farms partially down; the corners choked with sprouts, briars, and weeds; their barns and all the surroundings looking like desolation; the yard covered with bits of rails and lumber; the gates out of repair and dragging; their wagons old, rough, and broken; their plows, hoes, shovels, forks, etc., quite rusty—some in and round the barn, others over the farm in the fence corners—anywhere and everywhere being with them their proper places. Again, quite too many of our farmers who are in easy circumstances *appear* in the towns and at public gatherings as *paupers*, wearing coarse, rough, and broken apparel, in uniform with their wagons and harness. This is the other extreme; this is not paying a due respect to themselves, nor to those with whom they mingle.

Such, indeed, is the character of too many men in the towns—such the character of a great many of our farmers; and I am truly sorry that I can say so much, having been myself a farmer in Montgomery county, Indiana, just thirty-five years. But after all this, I am proud to acknowledge that they are, as a class, our most industrious, useful, and respectable people; possessing withal more honesty and practical sense than a like number of the inhabitants of the towns. Yet they might be far more useful and respectable had they more regard for order and neatness in all they do— more regard for their *appearance* at home and abroad; and hence to hand down to their children and to posterity those ennobling and refining qualities, and less regard for hoarding up money and land, *land* and *money*, to be mostly squandered—to fall into the hands of sharpers and sharks soon after the accumulators have gone to their eternal rest.

What is true of one organ is equally so of all. The largest have the widest and longest range of comprehension with any people, and *vice versa*. Hence it is that a ceaseless growth or expanse of the brain, or of any organ of the brain, must necessarily widen and elevate one's range of ideas, and make him progressive. And progression is no less than self-improvement.

And finally, he who would make good progress in self-improvement, and be a man, and not a mental slave, must have a mind so liberal and so bold as to dare think for himself; and hence, to investigate both sides of every subject, and to speak his sentiments on all proper occasions; as to dare do right under all circumstances, "not minding what people will say"—not minding how many shallow heads and wise heads, saints and sinners, may become displeased with him; "for if God (the Right) be for us, who can be against us?"

CHAPTER VIII.

HIS SELF-RESPECT AND LIFE-TIME DUTIES.

Every person has some sort of an opinion, more or less distinct, of all persons with whom he is acquainted. This opinion may embrace intellect, disposition, virtues, vices, personal appearance, deportment, condition in life, etc. So, also, every one has some opinion of himself on the same, and upon many other subjects, best known to himself.

When one examines himself, he seems to do it as though he were another person; he uses the eyes of others. He turns aside, as it were, by the way, to see himself pass by. The judgment which he forms of himself is generally much more unsound than that which he forms of others; for the eye can not see itself; so neither can any man see himself. He must use a mirror, and there are many of these—books, history, daily example, every person with whom he comes in daily contact, his own experience, etc. If he sees himself in these, and thereby corrects his own errors and follies, and gives himself reasonable and just credit for his attainments, he may come at last to be entitled to entertain a respect for himself. There is a certain best thing to be done, and a certain best manner of doing it in all possible circumstances in which one may find himself. Nothing is entitled to be considered best or just, which does not conform to natural law. To that best thing, and to that best manner, no one, perhaps, ever perfectly attains; but it can not be doubted that there is some such standard, and he who comes the nearest to it, is *he* who is best entitled to entertain a good respect for himself. There are some persons who seem to have had this standard in view throughout their lives; while the great majority seem to merely stumble and float along as if they had never even thought of any such principles or rules of action—as if they had no right or necessity to think for themselves—as if it were sufficient for them to think and to act as certain other people think and act.

But the truth is, *man* was created for action—created to think and to act for himself—to be the arbiter of his own destiny—to save himself, and to perpetuate and elevate his dear race. His actions were intended to enable him to secure good to himself; and good to himself depends upon the performance of his duties to himself, to his family, to society, to his race. Duty to himself and to his country requires that he should improve his faculties—should avail himself of all the opportunities given to him for that purpose. The hours, then, which are permitted to slide by without any improvement are forever lost; and in so losing them he breaks a moral law and must suffer for it.

Apply this to the vocations in which one is to cultivate his mind in any business, mechanical or literary. When any one sees himself surpassed by others and left far in the rear; when he is called upon to measure himself against another; and when he sees that comparisons are made between him and others, greatly to his disadvantage, he may feel, and most men do feel, that they are thus depreciated because the precious time which was allotted to improvement has been passed in trifling amusements, or in idle pursuits. To some minds the suffering from such causes is extremely acute. The bitter rememberance which they have of the past, as connected with the present and the future, is the punishment for breaking a positive law. They may console themselves, perhaps, with the firm resolution that they will repair the wrong done in the past time by diligence in the time to come; but they find that time brings with it its own demands. They are fortunate, indeed, if they can do in one space that which belongs to it, and also that which belongs to another, and in another season of life.

One can hardly say correctly that his time is his own, and that he may dispose of it as he pleases. His time is his life. It is given to him in trust, and like other trustees he will be held to an account, in which there is no possibility of concealment, and where nothing will depend on proof; and also, it may be supposed that his conscience will some day say to him, as he reviews his past career:

"There was confided to your use a term of time, and you knew, or could have known, the laws prescribed to you in performing your trust; then have you come from that trust to render an account burdened with self-reproach, and with marks of guilt which you can not hide; or are you come without any advancement in the knowledge of your duties, and with no other account than that your days rolled by in boyish pursuits or useless and profligate amusements, but little wiser now, when you have about done with the world, than when you left the cradle of infancy? Or are you come with the exalted acquirements which you might have, and with that innocence and purity which you would have, if you had obeyed the laws of your nature? Where have you read in these laws that no duties to yourself and to your associates were enjoined upon you? Have you not been told by every breath you drew, by every movement of your frame, by every thought of your mind, by every just pleasure that you have had, by every pang that you have suffered, and by all that you have been capable of perceiving and learning, that there were laws or rules of action laid down to you as your unerring guide in the discharge of your sacred trust, and that an account of your stewardship would finally be exacted?"

CHAPTER IX.

SOCIAL RIGHTS AND DUTIES.

On this subject many fanciful theories have been given to the world. The ancient poets represented mankind as at first in a state of innocence and happiness during what is termed the golden age, and as declining gradually into vice and misery through the silver, brazen, and iron ages. The Bible also informs us that at the commencement of our race, man was perfect. Some dreamers have imagined solitude in the cave and forest to be the natural condition of man, and have attributed most of the evils which afflict humanity to the institution of society and private possessions.

The great error of such theorists is, that they assume the mind to be altogether passive—to have no spontaneous activity giving origin to wants or desires; and ascribe the formation of almost all our propensities and tastes to the situation in which they were first manifested

A more rational view of the origin of society suggests the idea, that man, having been endowed with natural aptitudes and desires, founds upon these every institution which has been universal among mankind; therefore, the origin of society is to be attributed to the social principle.

What, then, is the solution that human nature, properly understood, presents to us? It shows that man possesses mental faculties endowed with spontaneous activity, which give rise to many desires equally definite with the appetite for food; and that among these faculties are several which act as social instincts, and from the spontaneous activity of these, society has obviously been proceeded.

The gregarious instinct or propensity in mankind to congregate, shows that human nature dictates that we should live in the social state, as we can not otherwise act in obedience to the requirements of our mental nature, any more than we can support our physical constitutions without food and sleep. Of what use would the power of speech be to the solitary being? Without combination, what advance could be made in science, arts, or manufactures? As hunger is adapted to food, aud the sense of vision to light, so is society adapted to the social faculties of man; indeed, the presence of human beings is indispensable to the gratification and excitement of our mental powers in general, for what a *void* and *craving* is experienced by those who are cut off from communication with their fellows. Persons who have been placed in remote and solitary stations on the confines of civilization have uniformly become dull in intellect, shy, unsocial, and unhappy.

In some one of our prisons, the criminals are allowed to work together during the day, but are strictly prohibited from speaking or otherwise communicating with each other; yet the very presence of their companions is found to sustain the social faculties, so that their health is not greatly impaired.

The balmy influence of society on the human mind may be discovered in the vivacious and generally happy aspect of those who live in the bosom of a family or mingle freely with the world; while the chilling effect of solitude is apparent in the cold, starched, and stagnated manners and expression of those who refrain from associating with their fellow-creatures. A man whose muscular, digestive, respiratory, and circulating systems greatly predominate in energy over the nervous system, stands in less need of society to gratify his mental faculties than an individual oppositely constituted; he delights in active muscular exercise, and is never so happy as with the elastic turf beneath his feet and the blue vault of heaven over his head. But where the brain and nervous system are most energetic, there arise mental wants which can be gratified only in society, hence a residence in a town or city is felt indispensable to enjoyment; the mind flags and becomes feeble when not stimulated by collision and converse with kindred spirits. In short, the social state is plainly as natural to man as it is to the bee, the raven, or the sheep. This question, then, being set at rest, the duties implied in the constitution of a society are next to be considered. The first duty imposed on man in relation to society is industry—a duty, the origin and sanction of which are easily discovered. Man comes into the world naked, unprotected, and unprovided for. He does not, like the brutes, find his skin clothed with a sufficient covering, but he must provide garments for himself; he can not perch on a bough or burrow in a hole, but must rear a dwelling to protect himself from the weather; he does not, like the ox, find his nourishment under his feet, but must hunt or cultivate the ground.

To capacitate him for the performance of these necessary duties, he has received a body fitted for labor and a mind calculated to direct his exertions, while the external world is adapted to his constitution. The too prevalent notion that labor is an evil, and rather a disgrace, must have arisen from the ignorance of the constitution of man, and from contemplating the effects of labor when carried to excess.

Labor, in the proper sense of the word, is exertion, either bodily or mental, for useful purposes. That man was intended by his nature to labor is evident, not only from the fact that very few gratifications are attainable without it, and a great many by its aid, but by the structure and laws of his constitution, which proclaim that active employment is essential to his welfare in every sense of the word—physically, mentally, morally, religiously, and socially. The misery and degradation of idleness has been a favorite theme of moralists in every age, and its baneful influence on the moral and bodily health has equally attracted the notice of the physician and of observers in general. Yea, there are this day millions upon millions literally dying off solely for the want of physical labor—many millions of them too idle or too proud to soil their hands, even to save their own lives. Indeed, happiness is nothing but the gratification of *active* faculties; and hence the more active our faculties are, and the more numerous those in agreeable action, the greater is the happiness which we enjoy.

But there can be no high, sustained, and healthy moral or spiritual life here on earth, except in connection with habits of *wise bodily* and *mental discipline;* because bad circumstances and influences can neither produce nor maintain good men; indeed, they furnish the seeds of good or evil, and man is but the soil in which they grow.

CHAPTER X.

HIS PECULIARITES AND VARIETIES.

'T is ignorance that binds people in chains;
'T is this, too, folly and fashion maintains.

Man in all ages of the world, in every clime, and on every isolated island, has possessed invariably the same cardinal elements of character; but, like all other animals, various and dissimilar in his colors, forms, languages, and mental peculiarities.

Yes, the God of Nature has made peculiarity and variety a fundamental law, for no two of his productions are exactly alike, and this law is invariably observed throughout his whole domain.

Through all grades of existence, from the lowest animalcule to the most magnificent universe sweeping through space, peculiarity and variety illimitable is stamped upon all.

Similarity may exist superficially, yet dissimilarity inheres in all substantially.

The leaves on the trees, the flowers in the valleys, the sands on the coasts, the fowls of the air, the hosts of worlds which fill the immensity of space—all exist with a specific peculiarity and variety in all their phenomenal manifestations.

The mineral kingdom may be grouped into species—the animal classified into races, families, types, or genus; yet these are broken up into endless subdivisions, which run off into an infinitude of varieties. Mankind also exists in types, races, and families. The types are as distinct in their external phenomena as color can possibly make them. Their organization of brain, their mental characteristics, their languages, habits, and all the non-essentials to existence present the same peculiarities and varieties.

Every animal has its individual character; every man has something distinguishing in form, proportions, countenance, voice, and gesture—in feelings, temper, and thought. Our notions, opinions, likes, dislikes, tastes, and talents are as various and dissimilar as our faces and persons. And this variety is the source of everything interesting and beautiful in the external world—the foundation of nearly the whole moral and social fabric of the universe.

Indeed, we are so constituted and related to each other, and to the surrounding objects and influences, that it is utterly impossible for us to think alike upon almost any subject.

And this fact, this wise providence, is certainly one of our greatest blessings, for without it there would soon be an end to all investigation, progress, and civil liberty.

Yet, strange to tell, that, on account of this highest blessing, we are, and have been, in all ages of the world, hating and persecuting each other. Yea, for no other cause the ancient nations visited each other with bloody wars and terrible desolations. Hence how low, foolish and unkind it is to proscribe and persecute our neighbors merely because they are not of our political party, not of " our church "—because they can not see through *our smoky and perverted glasses.* For it is not what we *may believe* or *profess* which makes us good or bad, but it is what we do—*what we do.* It makes no difference who raised the wheat, or where it grew; but the only question is, and must ever be, is it good wheat? Is it a merchantable article? Again, those who oppose a doctrine, creed, or institution do as much to maintain, build up, and perpetuate it as those who advocate it; for this opposition is merely a *necessary evil,* but which answers the same *important purposes* in society that the *cumbersome* brakes do on the trains, to prevent us running too rapidly, to excite, and to provide time for investigation—to avoid fatal reaction.

Yes, those who oppose us in politics, in religion, or upon any other subjects, are in the end our best friends and benefactors. They are our sentinels on the watch-tower while we sleep, and *vice versa.* For the world exists but by conflict, and is only maintained by opposition; we ever find one force pitted against another, and all things find their contrarieties to be the foundation of their preservation and their perpetuity.

Again, it matters not what may be the mere knowledge given to men, or the moral and religious precepts taught them, if the other circumstances by which they are surrounded be disregarded; because bad circumstances and influences can neither *produce* nor *maintain* good men; indeed, they furnish the seeds of good or evil, and man is but the soil in which they grow. Then—

> Why blame the thistles for having grown,
> After we ourselves the seeds had sown.

CHAPTER XI.

HIS MORAL EVIL.

God has planted in every evil the seeds of its overthrow and destruction.

"Fair truth! for thee alone we seek!
Friend to the wise, supporter to the weak;
From thee we learn whate'er is wise and just,
Wrongs to reject, pretensions to distrust."

A MAN'S reason is that faculty of the mind which enables him to distinguish truth from falsehood, and *good* from *evil*. It is the originator of all human society, of all governments, and of all true religion; and to the tribunal of reason *he* should bring all questions, whether they are said to be divine or human; and if they will not stand a fair, honest, and common sense approval, he should adjudicate accordingly and throw them out of court. Therefore, in order to properly examine a question of such great importance as "whence cometh moral evil," and one on which so many conflicting opinions have been entertained in all ages of the world, we should be governed by "fair truth," reason, and common sense; we should consider *man* as he really is, a natural being, governed, affected, and controlled solely by *natural* laws. Hence we must contemplate our species as they are sent into the world, almost entirely destitute of every kind and degree of knowledge, but endowed with mental faculties susceptible of improvement and continual progression.

We are also endowed with innate appetites and passions, which were intended to answer the very best purposes when under the control of *reason*, by which means their impulsive operations are restrained within due bounds and directed to proper objects. There are also proper objects destined to act upon these appetites and passions, which may be called motives or incentives to action; and were we to be divested of these appetites and passions, and the objects withdrawn which are destined to act upon and excite them, we should be as useless in creation as a ship without sails or rudder.

When we are excited by these means to the performance of any good and necessary act, we do our duty and incur no penalty; but when the excitement leads to a breach of law, it is a wrong act, and the perpetration criminal, being calculated to produce disorder, strife, and misery. Under these circumstances we are placed here at school, to learn laws, to acquire an experimental knowledge of the nature and consequences of just and honorable actions, and also of physical, moral, and social evils, by which means we may finally be convinced that without obedience to laws it is impossible to be healthy, prosperous, and happy, or to live out our allotted time, to fill our mission here on earth, and that degredation and suffering are the *natural, necessary,* and inevitable consequences of lawless actions.

And, on the contrary, that well-doing, happiness, and longevity are the *natural* results invariably following the exercise of industry, prudence, justice, and benevolence; hence every man in society is amply rewarded for all his good works and punished equivalently for all his bad works. Again, all mankind are *naturally* endowed with a large amount of self-love, and prone to live almost entirely for themselves, regardless of the rights of others.

They were also created with many wants and desires, and it was *equally* unnatural for them to *willingly* labor to gratify and supply these wants and desires; therefore, not being content with the comforts produced by their own industry, they coveted those of their more worthy fellow-men. Now the strong rose up against the feeble to take from them the fruits of their labor; the feeble united with other feeble to oppose their violence.

And the strong said, why worry ourselves to produce the necessaries of life which we can find in the hands of others? Therefore, let us unite and dispoil them; they shall produce for us, and we will live without toil. Now, those uncontrolled appetites and passions having assumed a thousand different forms, the strong united for oppression, and the feeble for self-protection; men mutually robbed and tormented each other, thereby producing oppressors and the oppressed, the rich and the poor, the master and the slave, until universal discord, strife, and misery have spread all over the world, and so long as the causes—*ignorance* and *cupidity*—shall reign supreme, as they now do, the mischievous and degrading effects can never cease.

CHAPTER XII.

HIS PENALTIES.

Man has ever been a rebellious animal, living in daily violation of the sacred laws of his being, an enemy practically to himself, to his family, and to his race; fastening on them, by entailment and otherwise, untold troubles and afflictions. But this state of things was, to a great extent, unavoidable, and even necessary, to teach the people those laws and the penalties attached to them necessary to preserve and to restrain them.

For if the young, or even the aged, could revel in dissipation and crime with impunity, when and where would they stop? When would they ever cease to do evil and learn to do good? And when would they ever even think of laws? Never! And it is a self-evident fact, that no man can *possibly* find a true and lasting interest in doing a wrong act against his country or his fellow-man, for just so sure as he does a wrong act—violates any one or more of nature's laws, the laws of his being, or of society—just as sure will suffering, *consequent*, sooner or later, overtake him or his posterity, or both. Because this suffering is as inseparable from crime as an effect is from its cause; is blended in the very nature of things—in the constitution of those wise and benevolent laws—and which is, and ever must be, in strict proportion to the transgression. Without this suffering upon the infraction of laws, we never could have learned them nor the penalties attached to their violation; never could have progressed in civilization and refinement; never could have properly appreciated anything; never could have risen higher in the scale of animated nature than the common animal.

It is true we learn many of those laws from books and observation; *but some bodies had first to learn them by suffering the penalties incident to their violation, or else they never could have been learned.*

And it was made possible, and even convenient, under proper discipline, to so learn and to appreciate those laws, that by maturity we might be wise and prudent enough the rest of our lives to live measurably in obedience to them, and thereby avoid to a great extent that long catalogue of troubles and afflictions which overtake so very many of the human family.

But it seems that every man's cup must be mixed with joys and sorrows, for we are surrounded with temptations; and the great store-house from which we *have* to draw our pittance is filled with both healthful and poisonous viands intermixed, and every man has to be his own druggist, that he may so mix his cup as to suit his peculiar temperament and appetite; and in so compounding, when he unfortunately poisons himself, as multiplied millions do, the consequences are his own.

But everything *must have* its opposite; the one implies the other; the one as necessary as the other. Nor can we fully estimate the one without first realizing the other; we must suffer from the one to greatly enjoy the other. Hence, it is obvious that it was in the plan of

Deity, that man from infancy to maturity, at leats, must *necessarily* and *unavoidably* violate laws that he might learn laws—that he might learn practical life—that he might learn enough of men and things to perpetuate and to elevate his race. And which knowledge could be acquired by having, as before said, to suffer the pains and penalties incident to the infraction of laws, and, also, in being allowed the manifold and unspeakable blessings consequent upon living in obedience to them.

And the great beauty and utility of this divine plan is, that these two opposite forces act upon us as incentives to obey laws; the former repels us from the wrong; the latter attracts us to the right. This is the way, the only way, that our great Preceptor has to teach us these laws, and to induce us to live in obedience to them.

We are his pupils from infancy until our decease; and all our trials, troubles, and afflictions are but so many kind lessons imparted to teach us wisdom, justice, benevolence, and humanity.

Then it would seem from the foregoing, that man, notwithstanding his foibles and misgivings, is *all right as created;* from the fact he possesses no mental attribute, no appetite or passion, which is not *indispensably* necessary to his well-being when properly controlled and directed by intelligence.

But *this man* can only act from what he knows; nor can he learn anything only through the medium of his five physical senses: hearing, smelling, feeling, tasting, and seeing. Now if these senses be feeble or uncultivated, and he remains too ignorant to know the laws of his being and of society, how is he to obey them? Indeed, *ignorance* is the great sin—the primitive cause of nearly all suffering and crime—for every man loves himself well enough to desire happiness.

The mind of a child is like unto a sheet of fair paper, on which everybody except himself is allowed to scribble. He no more makes his own mind and character than he does his person; therefore, his future must be just what entailment and education make him.

Hence, the present unfortunate condition of the masses who float along on the ocean of human opinions without compass or rudder—left to the mercy of their tempestuous passions, with no other guide than unskillful pilots, ignorant of their course and whither they goeth.

Yes, man is truly a creature of circumstances. His country, his parents, entailments, education, and religion are all matters over which he has no control; if he had been born in Turkey, he would have been a Mohommedan; in Hindostan, a Brahmin; and in China, a Buddhist—would have consulted the sticks of fate.

Verily, he only acts as he is acted upon; and ever in obedience to the one or to the other of the two great forces, attraction and repulsion, between which he ever vibrates. Indeed, the poor fellow has to run the gauntlet all the days of his life.

These propositions are as true and invariable as the needle to its pole, or as the laws which govern cause and effect; then why *slander man*, as being by nature base and vile, and in the very next breath deify him as being the creator and director of his mind, character, and destiny. Nor should we denounce and despise the poor, ignorant, and reckless because they are so; from the fact their condition has been forced upon them by entailment, education, monopoly, and superstition—by laws and institutions not in harmony with human nature, divine justice, love and mercy.

> Why blame the thistle for having grown,
> *After we ourselves the seeds had sown?*

CHAPTER XIII.

HIS ACTIONS ARE THE RESULTS OF CIRCUMSTANCES.

I NOW propose to discuss the doctrine expressed in the above caption, but in so doing will be compelled to tread upon controverted ground; but, nevertheless, am aswell satisfied of the truth of the proposition as I am of the truth of the plainest mathematical axiom. It is not only true as regards the actions of men, but it is equally true of every kind of action, whether physical, moral, or social, throughout the whole kingdom of nature. It is a well-established theory that all bodies occupying infinite space, whether organic or inorganic, animate or inanimate, move or act in obedience to one of two great fundamental or primary forces, namely, attraction or repulsion; that one or the other of these two forces must be greater than the other, otherwise no action can be produced. This theory will be admitted to be true as regards physical action. Then the only question is, is this theory also true as regards moral action? It evidently is. For example, whenever an individual is prompted to do an act, whether it be of a moral or social nature, there are always present with the person, in his mind, two antagonistic principles, generally termed a *will* and a *nill*, corresponding with I *will* and I *will not*. Or, in other words, the person is influenced or acted upon by an *inclination* and a *disinclination* to do the thing contemplated; and whatever the individual finally does in the premises is invariably in obedience to the greater of these two contending forces.

The proportional strength, character, quality, etc., of these two forces, depend and rest upon the immediate anterior circumstances of the individual at the time the act was done.

How many, or what the precise character, the combinations, etc., of these circumstances that underlie and constitute the cause of all human actions *are*, is not within the knowledge or capacity of any one to say or describe; yet we can obtain a knowledge of some, or even many of the circumstances that induce us to do and to act as we do.

Another truism is, that there never *are*, nor can be, two circumstances precisely alike; consequently no two persons can be placed in exactly the same circumstances, on the same principle that two bodies can not occupy the same place at the same time.

Now for an illustration. I will take two persons, A. and B., who live in the same town. A. is a strict member of a popular church; believes our Bible to be the revealed will of God, but that all others are the productions of ignorant or designing men, consequently of no use to the world.

Believes there is a heaven to gain and a hell to shun in a future state of existence, and that the only road to that heaven is through the *church*, which he attends regularly, and prays feelingly (the more we feel the less we reason).

He has an exalted idea of his own wisdom and piety; condemns and consigns to an endless hell all who *have* to differ with him in opinion; looks upon infidels (so-called) or liberalists, and their principles, as extremely immoral and dangerous, consequently has but little sympathy and affiliation for them.

On the contrary, B. is a liberalist, and believes all bibles, churches, creeds, theories, and institutions to be good and useful in their *day;* hence can cheerfully fraternize and commune with all the sects and peoples of the earth, because he believes them all equally sincere and honest in their views and pretensions, acting alike from the best evidences in their possession—*from the influences of entailment and education.*

He respects the opinions and even the prejudices of all persons and creeds; hates not nor persecutes even the brawling and presumptive hypocrite, but merely pities such, because they are the imbecile creatures of unfortunate entailment and education, " knowing not what they do." He has no desire to ever realize a future heaven unless the lowest and meanest of his race can enjoy it as well as himself—all in their proper spheres or mansions ("In my Father's house are many mansions"*), according to the everlasting and all-pervading laws of affinity and affiliation, there to progress onward and upward forever more. Denies the existence of a future hell, and believes it to be a mere myth, a relic of ancient paganism, a doctrine at war with all his ideas of infinite wisdom and goodness. He regards all men of every class, condition, and occupation, as equally useful and necessary in promoting the intelligence, virtue, prosperity, and happiness of their Creator's people as a

---

* John, chapter 14, verse 2.

whole—all equally worthy and exalted before him, for "Peter said, Of a truth I perceive that God is no respecter of persons."*

Denies, also, that the principles of the liberalists are dangerous; that they are anything else than moralizing and reformatory, from the fact they study, adore, and teach the great laws of nature which govern men physically and mentally, morally and socially; try to learn something of mental and moral science, something of themselves, that they may know how to sympathize and indulge their neighbors; that they may rise above all this low persecution and slang so common among very many people who consider themselves worthy and respectable.

And, lastly, they believe that the only sure and safe way to secure happiness and salvation *here* and *hereafter* is to do right—to be industrious, frugal, honest, kind, and truthful—*to deal fairly with all people*—in short, to live every day in practical obedience to the physical, moral, and spiritual laws of our being.

Now, these two men being equally honest in their opinions, what is the cause of the difference of their views on this important subject? Evidently nothing but different circumstances. As before stated, it is impossible to particularize, but we can generalize.

The first general circumstance that I shall notice is their different training or education. Secondly, the organization of the contentes of their craniums is very different. The particular organization of the mentality of A., together with the natural quality and combination of his mental faculties or organs, modified by education,

---

*The Acts, chapter 10, verse 34.

with other unknown circumstances, in the aggregate, constitute the natural and legitimate cause of just such results as I have before noticed in regard to the particular character of A. So, likewise, the particular character of B. has for its cause a particular combination of natural and appropriate circumstances.

Now, how can these men, living in and surrounded by such stern, invincible, and overwhelming circumstances, constituting absolute causes, avoid the natural, necessary, and inevitable results? If they can, then a particular cause can exist without its particular effect, which is absurd.

Therefore, it is clear that all men act according to circumstances, and can no more avoid doing *just as they do than an effect can exist without a cause;* but, nevertheless, they are, for their own good, for their preservation and instruction, responsible to all the laws of their being and society.

Indeed, I see an inexorable necessity which produces and governs all things. The rain falls and wind blows, the sun shines or it is obscured by clouds, simply because neither of them can help it. In the moral world there are other disturbances on precisely the same principle.

The American revolution, the war of 1812, and the late war between the North and South were brought about by unavoidable circumstances. So in the life of every individual the same law obtains. Unrelenting necessity, like a sheriff, pursues us through all our existence.

We have no choice, strictly speaking, in anything. We are carried along like the *mighty waters* and the *myriads of planets*, by the inexorable and everlasting laws of necessity—by circumstances.

It is true we have a will, but then it is always controlled by the two great forces, attraction and repulsion, as aforesaid—by circumstances; and so there is no choice.

If there were, then there would be free agency, which is impossible. For instance, if B. were a free agent, he could become a Christian, but he can't so choose, because the evidence (which he did not make) is right the other way; hence he is a liberalist.

Byron once said that men are the sport of circumstances. The more I see of human actions, the more I am convinced that this saying is correct.

The philosophy of life seems to be about this: If a child happen to be the offspring of what phrenologists call a legal and prudent marriage—happen to possess favorable physical and mental entailments, and is properly trained to industry and economy, and educated to know and to appreciate the laws of his being and of society, and is put to some useful business, and meets with no great misfortunes—he will have a happy and respectable existence, and *vice versa*. But in either case he is the creature of circumstances. We are forced into life, forced through it, and forced out of it; and all along the journey, from the cradle to the grave, there is not a moment, as it appears to me, in which we are not controlled by circumstances. I look upon human nature as it is, and see in it the verification of Robert Owen's great philosophical and social problem, "The character of man is made for him, and not by him."

Now, if the above propositions be not correct, how

and whence comes all this ignorance, poverty, crime, degradation, and misery in the world? Do any choose to be so? No. Then why are they so? Because they could not help it. Circumstances made them what they are, and this is the reason of their wretchedness.

Again, it is a self-evident fact that all men love themselves well enough to desire happiness; therefore, it is contrary to all we know of human experience to suppose mankind sincerely loves *ignorance, poverty,* and *misery,* as it would be to suppose that they really prefer *blindness* to seeing, hunger to food, and *sore affliction to happiness.*

Then what are the lessons to be derived from this kind of philosophy? Wisdom and benevolence—two of our noblest qualifications. The first teaches us the vast importance of observing the great and *sacred* laws of marriage, of entailments, and of surrounding our offspring with proper circumstances, which, taken together, *fix* and *determine* the future character and destiny of our children.

It also teaches the beneficence of our Creator in having blessed us with such a law, by which we are enabled to elevate and refine our dear race, and consequently to lessen, to a vast extent, the misery and crime incident to human society. The second admonishes us *not* to persecute and proscribe our neighbors on account of their opinions—not to withdraw our sympathies from the wretched and degraded on account of their poverty and wretchedness; because circumstances made them what they are, and because, also, a variety of things, opinions, and classes ever have existed, and must *necessarily* and *unavoidably* ever exist, from the fact it is the order and arrangement of nature. But we should rather have compassion for those who are, as we suppose, more ignorant, destitute, and impious than ourselves, and lend them our influence and assistance to better their condition—should rather endeavor to establish such circumstances as shall secure universal *mental* liberty and social happiness.

CHAPTER XIV.

HE IS HELD IN THE ARMS OF NECESSITY FOREVER.

"Happy is the man who, studying nature's laws,
Through known effects can trace the secret cause."

THE operations of nature and the actions of men are nothing more than certain causes producing certain effects by an inevitable necessity. And behind any effect there *must* be a cause superior to the effect, nor can any effect be produced without an act; and behind every act there *has to be* a power superior to the act produced; and so far as I can see, the cause of every act is spontaneous, and that spontaneous causes lie back beyond the control of human will. *Every act is an effect*, and is part and parcel of the constitution of the physical universe, which constitution is self-acting; and so far as I can go with my philosophy, may safely say that the universe is self-sustaining and self-directing in its magnitude, and in its minutia no less. This universe, in its various workings, in its tangible effect, in its occult causes, in all its great things and in all its little things, in every property and condition, I call *nature;* and all the doings of nature, from her yet undiscovered workings in minutia, reaching out to magnitude yet ungrasped, I call the works of necessity; and I call this work the work of necessity because it can not be otherwise.

Things must be as they *are*, because the hidden causes of nature make them as they are.

Invisible, inevitable laws govern creation, acting through men as well as things, and the only murmur in the wide domain of creation that breathes an utterance *questioning* nature's perfect jurisdiction is from vain and fragile man, who declares he *do n't*, but really does, obey nature's laws *perfectly*, from the cradle to the grave; and he obeys them because he *must*, because he is held in the arms of necessity forever. Yes, he obeys them from the fact it was, as before said, in the plan of Deity that he should not only obey them, but that he should *necessarily* and *unavoidably* violate them in order that he might learn them—that he might learn wisdom—that he might learn his own weakness and dependence; hence to be induced to feel for others. Indeed, it appears that suffering and toil is the price of our tuition and happiness; for he who infringes laws must suffer in proportion to the transgression.

He who *will not*, or *can not*, read and think for himself is not allowed to progress much in wisdom—is not allowed to enjoy the rich blessings derived from that source; and he who *will not* toil to secure the comforts of life shall not eat.

Again, men, like the planets, are controlled and kept in their orbits or spheres by the two great and primary forces, attraction and repulsion; and to illustrate this proposition further, I will suppose two persons, A. and B. The former is reputed the best man in town, and the latter the worst one. But these two men wield an equal influence in promoting the good of society; because A. (best class) invites, attracts the youth and the aged to rise up toward him; while B. (lowest class) with equal force repulses them toward first class—from vice and crime—from evil. Yet this hateful thing called *evil* has availed as much in making us what we *are* as good has done; from the fact we are not only attracted, but *driven* to the good, to justice and fair dealing, from the fear of *evil*—from the fear of suffering.

Suppose, again, that C. and D. wish to move a lot of horses to a distant pasture, but they (like most men) will not toil (only) nor yet drive; therefore, C. goes ahead with a bunch of fodder and calls—attracts—while D. follows after, whip in hand, and drives—repulses. And thus the object is attained, and thus do all men, from *necessity*, strictly obey nature's laws.

And lastly, as a further illustration on this point, I will here draw a line and place E. and F. at the center of it. Now E. goes off to the right, obeys law, and does well. F. goes to the left, disobeys law, and suffers for it; but, nevertheless, does well too—well for himself, as he thereby learns law—learns to do so no more; and well for his neighbors, because it is from other people's blunders and misfortunes that we learn our best lessons—learn caution—learn how to avoid troubles and ruin.

Yes, it is mostly from this suffering (for crime) and from such lessons that we learn our relations and obligations to other men—learn our own *ignorance* and *nothingness*—learn humility and sympathy; and but for such agencies, we would be destitute of wisdom, justice, and humanity—would not be fit to live on the earth.

Hence I have shown that we do really obey nature's laws *perfectly* from the cradle to the grave; that all our acts are in harmony with her laws, and promote, sooner or later, our own best interest, and the good of others.

Again, every man would be rich and famous; but of necessity almost every one is poor and without fame.

No man would go a begging, but necessity often compels men to beg; because they are, in their physical and social capacity, placed under the rigid law of necessity, both in things external and in their actions; but to themselves they seem to be free, and they are free to act according to the *motives* and *forces* which determine their choice.

Man is held by the laws of nature in every deed he does, just as surely and securely as he is held down to the ground by the weight of his body—by law of gravitation; yet, notwithstanding, he is, for his own best interest, amenable to all the laws of his being and of the community; for pain and woe are the natural and necessary concomitants incident to their infringement.

Oppression and injustice are rife in the land, not because men are willing them to be, but because they *must be.* Inhuman deeds, merciless slaughter, universal murder, pains and woe unmeasured, human hands deal out to human beings. Why? Not because of human will, but because of unavoidable, inevitable necessity. (A fatal necessity sports with the lot of mortals.)

All acts, whether they are called natural or unnatural, are the lawful productions of nature; and all productions are natural, whether they are called unnatural or artificial.

There is no instinct, no desire, no belief, no unbelief, no love, no hate, no persuasion, which does not hold a place in nature's bosom. There are no acts which men and women do that are not done in nature, and by nature's inflexible workings. All acts are natural, and being natural, are unavoidable, are a necessity; and a necessity is something above the power of human volition and human action; hence man, in all his acts, is held in the arms of necessity forever.

Are not tornadoes and earthquakes, excessive rains, excessive droughts, etc., etc., above and beyond the control of human will? If they are not, why are they not averted?

Are not human wars that prostrate human successes, prosperity, and happiness—that desolate so many happy homes, and carry agony to every hearth—above human control? If they are not, why are they are not avoided?

Are not all the hateful things of life above the power of human volition to control? If not, why are there so many in the world? The answer is, because they are above the power of man to control; hence whatever is, is a necessity, or else things would not be.

Some say that joy and happiness, and all the lovely things of life, come to us because we desire them; because our volition leads us to do that which commands them.

They may think so, and no doubt it appears so to those who have not carefully examined the subject; but they are, nevertheless, of actual necessity, and not the fruits of human will, because they come of a power that is back of and superior to human will.

And thus, too, is man, in all his *joy* and *prosperity*, as well as in all his *adversity*, held in the arms of necessity forever—acting only as he is acted upon.

Then, what instruction may be derived from the foregoing illustrations? Nothing of an immoral or irreligious nature, I am sure, for if such be man, as it surely is, we should desire, above all other considerations, to learn the fact, that we may the better know how to train him—how to respect his opinions and prejudices—how to make the proper allowance for his ignorance and misgivings—how to elevate and refine him, and how to truly christianize him. But if such be not man, certainly our learned ones will be kind enough to explode my sophistry that the good people may suffer no serious violence.

Now, having gone through with my arguments, and clearly proven, as I think, the doctrine contained in the above caption, will come to a close, and with the confidence that no honest and reflecting man will accuse me of tolerating immorality or crime; for I say again, as I have before said in this essay, that no person can find a true and lasting interest in doing a wrong act—that transgression and suffering are inseparable—that all our debts of sin *must* be settled by the first to the fourth generations, and that there *can not* be any possible escape this side of the grave.

CHAPTER XV.

HIS CONFLICTING ELEMENTS AND OPPOSING FORCES HARMONIZED.

'May we learn to kindly disclaim
The narrow view, the selfish aim;
And with a manly zeal embrace
Whate'er is friendly to our race."

MAN has ever been and now is a restless, selfish, inconsistent, and illiberal being, finding fault with and persecuting his fellow-men for mere imaginary wrongs; finding fault with all his surroundings, with the physical elements, and even with the God who made him. Yet,

"Did we but strive to make the best
Of troubles that befall us,
Instead of meeting cares half way,
They would not so appall us.
Earth has a spell for loving hearts,
Why should we seek to break it?
Let's scatter flowers instead of thorns—
The world is what we make it.

"If truth, and love, and gentle words,
We took the pains to nourish,
The seeds of discontent would die,
And peace and comfort flourish.
Oh! has not each some kindly thought?
Then let's at once awake it,
Believing that, for good or ill,
The world is what we make it?"

Nor is it surprising that he so unwisely deports himself, from the fact he is always looking at the dark side of everything—gazing on the one side of the picture, too lazy or too self-righteous and self-opinionated to even turn it over where he could see his neighbor as good as himself, and behold beauty, justice, benevolence, and *harmony* in all nature's works.

But everything must, as before said, have its opposite; the one implies and demands the other, producing necessary and endless contrasts, from which source we derive the greater part of our information. There is, the world over, just as much cold as heat; as much winter as summer; as much darkness as light; as much good as evil, and no more on the greater average, for everything in nature and in morals strives for and tends to the great and universal law of equilibrium.

The attainment and maintenance of this (health) equilibrium is man's ultimate and highest moral and social zenith; for his wisdom can not organize and perpetuate a state of society which will not *necessarily* and *unavoidably* carry along with it a certain amount of *evil* as well as good.

Then the great object or desideratum should be to see that the good shall greatly preponderate—that good shall hold the positive, and evil the negative.

This being, perhaps, more than communities generally do—*as much as nature's physical elements have ever done*—then why should we transient and imbecile mortals expect, in the enjoyment of our moral and social elements, to transcend in perfection the great I AM, who holds, as it were, in the palm of His hand millions of inhabited worlds. We can do as well without the calm as without the storm; as well without life as without death; and as well without good as without evil.

This evil is negative or undeveloped good;* it is a condition, force, or agency in nature, whose office it is to bring about, sooner or later, necessary results, being co-existent and equally necessary† with good, because we everywhere meet with evil incidently connected with agencies whose predominate and ultimate effects are beneficial. Indeed, everything we can think of is necessary. Yea, all institutions, theories, and creeds, either civil or religious, are good and useful in their day—the best that could be in their time devised and properly appreciated or enjoyed; but the world is progressing.

And yet, further, there is just as much universal intelligence and felicity produced from the one opposite as from the other, and both being necessary for the purification and equalization of our natural, moral, social, and religious elements—necessary for our perpetuation, happiness, and proper development; it requiring more or less of everything the mind can conceive, and twenty thousand and one things, ideas, and principles not yet discovered, to properly enlarge and develop the human mind.

Hence it is obvious that all classes of men, conditions, doctrines, creeds, goods and evils, wet and cold days, floods and storms, wars and rebellions, sickness and premature deaths, with all other troubles, trials, and afflictions, incident to human life, are (in their proper time

---

*Genesis, chapter 2, verse 17.   †Isaiah, chapter 45, verse 7.

and degree) highly beneficial to excite and promote our humanity and sympathy, our intelligence, happiness, and longevity. Consequently, the thing or principle called *evil* is nothing more at last than negative or undeveloped good or bad, but which is always present ("when I would do good, evil is present with me"*), influencing or controlling the actions of men.

That all flowers, bitter and sweet, contain more or less of honey; and that when we shall be philosophers enough to become, as it were, honey-bees, capable of extracting good, *present* or *future,* from all circumstances, creeds, and theories, then, and not until then, shall we ever enjoy our full measure of happiness.

Therefore, according to common sense, experience, and sound philosophy, there can not be in all nature anything wrong—all things, men, and circumstances being about as we should *now* expect them. Hence whatever is, is necessary.

And not only necessary in nature, but also in human society; yet whatever is in society can not always be right or expedient, *for it can not be morally right for one man to defraud another.* It was certainly wrong for S. A. Douglas and his co-workers to tear down the Missouri restriction, but it was highly necessary in order to arouse, to wake up, the then sleeping and servile North to a sense of her danger. Yea, even the outrages committed upon patriotic Kansas were very *necessary* to teach the people, both North and South, what slavery really was, what it could do, and what it would do—necessary to work up, to bring about the

---

*Romans, chapter 7, verse 21.

destruction of the "divine institution;" and, consequently, to create a greater affinity and affiliation between the people of the two geographical sections—to produce a unity of feeling, sentiment, and interest between them—to enable this government to take a high position among the first nations of the earth.

To illustrate: The terms, *right* and *wrong, good* and *evil*, can only be defined and known by the following standards, viz: All acts which are done in obedience to laws should be called right, and *vice versa*.

The terms, *good* and *evil*, are merely relative—the same as up and down; up at one time, being down at another, and *vice versa*. But all these acts which are necessary and fitly producing the greatest good to the greatest number, *present* or *future*, may be called good or necessary, and *vice versa*. For instance, the wicked act of Bonaparte in usurping the throne of Spain was the *necessary* and indirect cause of Mexico and South America becoming free republics.

And from the further consideration: If there were no dishonest men, there could be no honest ones; if there was no vice, there could be no virtue; if there was no slavery, there could be no freedom; if there was no darkness, there could be no light; and if there was no suffering, there could be no happiness, etc.

Therefore, how can we judge of the one thing only when contrasted with the other—with its opposite? How can we know the excellent but by contrasting it with the faulty? And this contrast is also one of the great sources of intelligence and pleasure.

Is not the pleasure of warmth derived from the previous cold? Could we enjoy food but for the previous hunger, or the cooling fountain but for the foregoing thirst?

Mankind know of no method of appropriating, or even of understanding any advantage or happiness, but by contrasting it with its opposite state or quality. The extremes only, long continued, appear to me as evils.

All these opposites are merely so many contrasts necessary to create variety, orders, and distinctions, making a world adapted to the wants and best interests of its inhabitants.

Then, worthy readers, would you have one endless sameness throughout creation? No *variety* and *peculiarity*, no difference in size or forms, no good, no evil, no sweet, no sour, no flowers, no thorns, no light, no darkness?

> No ignorance to overcome with wisdom?
> No poverty to overcome with plenty?
> No imperfection to transcend, and
> No suffering to teach the worth of happiness?

And if we had no *wars*, those omnipotent *teachers* and *regulators*, how could we estimate the great worth of peace, or what would prompt us to avoid strife and contention; and when would blind and *avaricious* man let go his hold on his fellow-man, and render unto Cæsar the things which are Cæsar's, and when would he *willingly* progress, although it is a law of nature that he *shall progress (slowly)* willing or not? Yes, he shall progress willing or not. And is it not far better that man should improve than that he should stand still at an unvarying point of morals and intelligence? I should decide in favor of improvement, considering progression, especially in intellectual acquirements, as the greatest source of pleasure which human life is capable of.

Now if this be so, imperfection and ignorance are necessary conditions; hence if we advance (as we must) on a scale, we have to commence from the lower end of it.

If we progress in knowledge, we must start from ignorance. If we increase in wisdom, there must have been a time of folly. And these lower conditions must have been attended with their consequences; and these consequences were the very stimulating causes of progress subsequently made, and even furnished the zest to its high enjoyment.

Indeed, I am quite unable to see how those imperfections could exist without their troublesome and painful consequences; or, indeed, what would be the advantages of improvement or progress but for these troubles and pains?

It is to avoid them that we seek improvement; that we strive after knowledge and perfection; in order that we may deliver ourselves from calamity and increase our happiness. This is the nature of all improvement.

Until railroads were invented, we could only travel by less desirable conveyances. Until printing was invented, we could not enjoy its advantages.

The steam engine was originally imperfect, and the consequences of that imperfection existed and stimulated to improvements; and but for those troubles, mishaps, and pecuniary losses consequent upon this imperfection, there never would have been any improvement; hence those losses to property and life, vexations, etc., were necessary evils—was negative or undeveloped good.

But as there are opposing forces and warring elements throughout all nature, so there are and needs to be in society; indeed, our social and religious institutions could not be perpetuated without approbation and disapprobation, merit and demerit, rewards and chastisements, and all those grades and distinctions now existing—it being only the abuses and excesses of our manifold blessings, of those grades and distinctions, goods and evils, vices and virtues, etc., about which the writer is complaining; for the greatest evils, as wars and rebellions, generally bring about among peoples and nations the rich blessings of emancipation, progression, justice, and equality.

Now, if we had no ignorance and imperfection to transcend, what use would we have for all our books, teachers, schools, and journals—for all our fine works on natural and moral philosophy—our colleges, bibles, preachers, etc., etc.? None at all.

If we had no poverty to overcome, what would excite us to industry, economy, emulation, and invention? And what would we be doing? We would, the most of us, if possible, be reveling in dissipation and crime—would be racing around day and night, annoying all civil and decent people; running in debt wherever credit could be found, hanging on us the richest costumes, riding in fine carriages, steamboats, and train coaches, gambling, drinking, etc., etc. In short, we would just go wild, and never find a stopping place until laid under the sod. Then a very large majority of the citizens of Thorntown and elsewhere should feel thankful that they are not rich—that they have no wealthy and indulgent parents to lean on—that they have to *save themselves*—that they *must* labor *steadily or starve.*

If we had no suffering from ill health and from other causes, how could we appreciate the blessings of life? What would excite in us benevolence and humanity for others in affliction, and what would there be to restrain us from unbounded licentiousness?

Yea, even our highest virtues, as benevolence and charity, when carried to certain excesses, produce great and lasting trouble and miseries.

And after we all shall have labored diligently and unitedly in suppressing the troubles and evils of society, *as we should do,* still there will remain enough and *too much* disorder and crime. We only need a more healthy equilibrium, but which never can be attained until society shall become more generally enlightened; never until the masses shall acquire self-reliance and moral courage enough to think and act for themselves upon all subjects and occasions; and hence to govern themselves more by natural laws, reason, and common sense.

All the above-named opposites, opposing forces, characters, and peculiarities are in accordance with nature, and necessary to constitute a harmonious whole; producing all those grades, distinctions, merits and demerits now existing in society, without which we could have nothing to stimulate us to industry, virtue, honor, or greatness.

No, not even the terms or ideas of good and evil, honest and dishonest, wise and unwise, noble and ignoble, could ever have entered the mind of man.

Hence ignorance, barbarity, and extinction would have been the inevitable doom of our tender race.

Now having gone through with my arguments under the various captions will come to a close, and leave the subject to abler pens that can treat it in a more becoming and scientific manner; particularly as I am well convinced that the reading public is not *now*, as a general thing, prepared to indorse many propositions or doctrines contained in this essay. But we should not expect to enjoy the fruit immediately after sowing the seed—not before it has time to mature; because society is progressing, the dark fogs will be dissipated, a greater light and salvation is coming, and it is but a poor philosopher who is not willing to wait—to wait fifty or a hundred years.

Then can we not learn, from the foregoing illustrations, to let our *reason* and *intuition* be the rule of our conduct, to carefully examine both sides of every subject, to turn the picture over and not forever look on the dark side of everything; to respect the opinions of our neighbors; and hence to cease our *intemperate* and unholy proscriptions and persecutions; to reconcile ourselves with the world as we *now* find it; to make peace with all mankind; to enjoy life under all circumstances; and finally to conclude, that—

"The world goes round and round,
  And the genial seasons run;
  And ever the right comes uppermost,
  And ever is justice done."

The following verses might be a further stimulus and prop to many of those philosophers who are capable of harmonizing their conflicting elements and opposing forces, to the end that they be enabled to enjoy life under all circumstances:

"I love the man who well can bear
  Misfortune's angry frown;
I love the soul that spurns despair,
  Though all his friends have flown.

"I love the soul so nobly proud,
  That misery can not blight;
The soul that spurns the jeering crowd,
  And sternly claims his right.

"I love that fortitude refined,
  Which sorrow can not break;
I love that strength of soul and mind,
  No earthly power can break.

"I love the man that scorns to bend
  Beneath affliction's blast;
Whose soul stoops not to foe or friend,
  Bound to truth till the last."

PART III.

CHAPTER I.

POSITION AND PRIVILEGE OF TRUTH SPEAKERS.

It seems to me there are three principal fundamental forms of the moral life, namely: active humanity, industry in acquiring knowledge, and honesty in imparting what we know. It is one of the highest duties of *man* to learn to know himself, and, secondly, to allow himself to be known; but the contending and false systems of the world are a great hinderance to simplicity of character and moral growth. The mathematician, the linguist, the geologist, the chemist, may be very wise in those matters which they have studied, but yet very bad moralists, and wholly incompetent to govern and educate man. The power to govern is in the knowledge of the nature of the thing governed. The mathematician may be a very bad reasoner on physiological matters, and the linguist no wiser for the ability to utter the same idea in several languages. If we would regulate our clock, we apply to a clock-maker; if we would regulate a steam-engine, we apply to the engineer; if we would cure a disease, we send for the physician; but if we would develop man's nature, and learn how to regulate his conduct, both as an individual and a member of society, would we send to Cambridge for a mathematician, or to Oxford for a linguist? "Man knows no more than he has observed;" but whose profession is it to observe the laws of man's nature and development? Physicians follow systems, take up their subjects only in parts; and to this day are disputing about the most ordinary diseases and the right method of cure, both as regards the physical conditions and the required phenomena. The homeopathic law—that "like cures like"—is doubtless a great truth, but certainly not the only principle of cure—nor of universal application. It is painful to see how every fresh application of a principle is twisted into a system—becomes a dogma, and hangs like a log about men's heels.

Physicians, again, remain ignorant of the most important facts in physiology, not clearly recognizing the principle that every part of a subject must be studied by itself, and also in relation to the whole, and the whole again in relation to a class of truths and to universal nature.

The body can not be understood when studied as a matter separate from its phenomenon, mind; nor mind irrespective of physical conditions, causes, and laws. The metaphysician, again, meditates upon his sensations and their sequence, and sees but in part, and very imperfectly, strangely unaware of the delusions to which he is subject; but could he even perceive correctly the whole phenomena of his thoughts and their order of development, it would only be like studying his bodily constitution by looking at himself in a glass; and he could tell us no more about the mind's action, the difference of men and the laws and causes of development, than the old Arab in the village can tell you in regard to medicine and the true nature and cause of diseases; and the metaphysician's mind is prejudiced and stuffed up by learning and abstract thought, and requires as much free air and ventilation as the Arab's cottage, and cleared of the cobwebs, will have to commence study afresh after another method. Man is the result of organization, the external circumstances acting upon this, and the force of knowledge. Plato was fully impressed with this, and his only hope for man was in producing good organizations, which were to be trained and developed under the most favorable circumstances; the whole to be regulated by a pure and practical morality and correct reasoning as a basis.

He would have the best men to govern, and would not allow the legislator to accumulate wealth or to marry; but would have his mind left as free as possible from all selfish considerations and temptations, from all influences likely to damage his love of truth, his honesty or desire for the general good.

And is it not the duty of every man to endeavor, above every other consideration, to know himself and the origin of his opinions; and hence to know his neighbor? "Know thyself," was the wise saying of Thales. "Bear and forbear," the constant admonition of Epictetus. In the confusion of opinions which now exist, and which seems likely to increase, I see no hope but in a thorough investigation of man's nature, the laws of his development, and the cause and origin of the opinions which he holds, and which men quarrel about, not seeing that their opinions are voluntary, and that, consequently, it is as great folly *to quarrel about our opinions as about the shape of our different noses.*

But I hear on every hand that men want the courage to speak the truth; that those who do declare their honest and full convictions often suffer in their worldly affairs, and find themselves stigmatized by the unthinking and self-righteous. This, I fear, is but too true; and which exhibits the demoralizing influence of our present systems of education. But surely to utter the truth that is within us dispassionately, and in pure affection, and for the general good, is most worthy of a good nature and as natural as the desire of freedom and the growth of beauty. To an honest mind, the courage would seem to be in the daring to secrete the truth, and to oppose the dictates of conscience and the free action of the mind.

Shall we be content to receive all the benefits of life, delighting in the free developing and beauty of nature, while we remain ourselves under a mask, and standing there a conscious criminal in the midst? For to disguise or deny what is true, is to live a lie—*is to live a lie*—being brave toward right and a coward toward men. But there are many persons, and most respectable, good, and pious persons, too, who have no faith in knowledge; in that faith of faiths, that rest for hope, that solace of grief; in that which so surely contributes to peace and peace of mind, to true wisdom and good works. And these persons talk of dangerous truths, us if all the dangers did not come from the side of ignorance and error; or as if any one truth could be opposed to any other truth, or to any system or faith founded on that which is true.

But no wise man will desire that any one thing be true in perference to another, nor that nature should stand still for his special gratification; and when he is in error will be most thankful for correction, and receive the news as gladly as if he had discovered a new truth. Nor must we forget that all conditions of things and opinions are right or necessary, and the best they can be in the time in which they exist—having their place in the plan of nature's progressive development. Again, that evil to individuals is universal good, and the calamities of life the occasion for magnanimity and the highest virtues.

Pain or pleasure, good or evil report, will follow as a consequence of our acts, but must never be the reason or motive of action; and men must be admonished that the recognition of philosophical necessity, or the sense of universal law, will not, as some suppose, set men loose from restraint to indulge their passions and evil desires.

These good people seem strangely possessed with notions of man's innate wickedness, forgetting that he has no mental attribute, appetite, or passion which is not indispensably necessary to his well-being when properly controlled and directed by intelligence.

But the reverse will be the fact; for a knowledge of the cause will give a reason for exertion and a confidence they did not possess before—will present a means to an end, and induce the application, acknowledging, in practice, a belief in moral results from sufficing causes. In a strange confusion of ideas, they neglect true fundamental causes and the study of the laws of man's nature and development, and even deny the existence of such laws. But none are to blame, though so many are in error; in error from want of knowledge and a clear unbiased mind, and a right method of inquiry. Nevertheless, we and kind must long continue to be injured in power and in peace by the operation of past ignorance, which has mournfully impaired the conditions of human life; but the emancipation which may be obtained is already precious beyond all estimate. Ignorant as we yet are, hardly able yet (even the wisest of men) to snatch a glimpse of the workings of nature, or to form a conception of the existence of law; obvious, as it is, that our condition is merely that of infant-waking upon the world of existence, the privilege of freedom, as far as we are now able to go, is quite inestimable. What a field it opens! What a prospect of ever-growing enjoyment to succeeding generations, in the development of the universe, under their contemplation! If we are daily sensible of the enjoyment of that "perpetual spring of fresh ideas," what must be the privilege of future generations, who shall, at the same time, be more naturally free to learn and find themselves in a bright noonday season of inquiry! It is truly cheering to think of. If we feel a contentment in our own lot, which must be sound, because it is derived from no special administration of our affairs, but from the impartial and necessary operations of nature, we can not but feel, for the same reasons, a new exhilaration on account of the unborn millions who will, ages hence, enter upon existence on better terms than those on which we hold it—contented as we are with our share of the good and the evil of human life.

It is a pleasant thing to have a daily purpose of raising and disciplining ourselves for no end of selfish purchase or ransom, but from the instinctive tendency to mental and moral health. It is a pleasant thing to be free from all arbitrary restraint in ministering to the good, great or small, of any who are about us. But what a thing it is to have, over and above all this, the conception of a future time, when all discipline will consist in a sweet and joyful surrender to nature, and all the forces of the universe will combine to lift man above his sorrows, to expand his old faculties and elicit new, and to endow him at once with all the good obtained by former generations, together with new accessions far beyond the compass of our thought! Nothing short of this seems to be the prospect of our race; and does it not shed back a light to our very feet, not only on high occasions of intercourse or meditation, but every day? ATKINSON, F. G. S.

TRUTH.

'Fair Truth! for thee alone we seek!
Friend to the wise, supporter to the weak;
From thee we learn whate'er is wise and just;
Evils to reject, professions to distrust,
Forms to despise, pretensions to deride,
And following thee, to follow naught beside."

CHAPTER II.

ORIGIN AND NATURE OF GOVERNMENT OF SOCIETY.

CONCERNING the origin of government various opinions have been held by philosophers. Some have regarded it as an extension of parental authority; others, as founded on compact between rulers and their subjects; while others give it a divine origin, and regard kings as the delegates of heaven, having a right to govern independently of the people. All these views appear unsound, for government arises directly from faculties inherent in human nature. Man is impelled by innate dispositions to live in society; he has a tendency to respect and obey those whom he considers his superiors; there is in him likewise a faculty which prompts individuals to assume authority and exact obedience; and from these natural tendencies government arises without any comprehensive design or compact whatever. In rude ages and nations, men with large active brains and considerable self-esteem and love of approbation would naturally take the lead, and be willingly obeyed by persons of feebler character.

This has been universally observed among children in all ages; and rationally viewed, government is the delegation to one or a few individuals of the power and authority of the nation, to be employed for the general good; and the only moral foundation of it is the general consent of the people who are to be governed. The notion of *right* in any one man, or class of men, to rule their neighbors for their own pleasure or advantage, against the inclination or contrary to the welfare of the subjects generally, is totally at variance with common sense, reason, and justice. This, however, does not imply that each individual is authorized to resist the government when it is disagreeable to his taste.

Before he can lawfully oppose or successfully improve it, he must succeed in convincing a large number of his fellow-subjects of its imperfections, this being necessary to secure their co-operation in providing a remedy, and till this be done he ought to continue his obedience. As soon as the evil becomes generally perceived, and a desire for its removal pervades the public mind, the amendment may easily be effected. Those who attempt to bring about changes, however beneficial, of public institutions, without a preparation of the public mind, encounter the hazard of being entirely baffled by the force of ancient prejudices and superstitions Nor is this an unwise arrangement of nature; for pure, moral institutions can not flourish unless the morality and intelligence of the people be correspondingly high; and hence improvements, even if accomplished before this condition be realized, would be speedily lost.

The grand aims of government are to secure the independence and freedom of the nation. A nation is independent when it is under the dominion of no foreign power; and a people are free when each individual of the state is completely protected, by just laws, from all arbitrary interference with his life, liberty, and property by his own government and his fellow-subjects. The history of the world shows that some nations live habitually under subjection to foreign powers; that other nations are independent but not free; and that only a very few, if any, enjoy alike freedom and independence. Of course, the best condition of a nation is when it is free as well as independent—that is, when it owns no master abroad, and when each individual acknowledges no master at home except laws consented to by the majority of the people and magistrates, who are themselves subject to the laws and merely their interpreters and administrators. Now, before a nation can attain this form of government, they must possess not only the qualities necessary for independence, but moral and intellectual gifts much higher than any which mere independence requires.

The love of justice must have become so prevalent, that no individual or limited number of individuals can muster followers sufficient to place himself or themselves above the rest. The community in general must be so far enlightened that they shall perceive the inevitable tendency of individuals to abuse unlimited power, and they must have so much of devotion to the general good as to feel disposed, by a general movement, when necessary, to resist and baffle all attempts at acquiring such dominion. As individuals, moreover, they must be, in general, moderate and just in their own ambition, and ready to yield to others all the political enjoyments and advantages which they claim for themselves.

Liberty, in short, can never exist except where intelligence and morality prevail among the great body of the nation to such an extent as to render them capable of restraining their own propensities within the limits of reason, and of pursuing objects related to the general welfare of the state.

Other philosophers again have contended that liberty consists in all men having the right to act as they may see fit, without any restraint or control whatever, except from the laws of nature. Now, I admit that a *rule* of this kind might answer in very many cases, yet, under all the circumstances in which we find people placed, it certainly would be a very unsafe one. There are, indeed, many men who go along as straight as a die, year after year, and behave correctly in all things, who are "a law unto themselves," and probably would be even if there were no statute laws; but, as there are so many people who go crooked and injure their neighbors, they must be restrained by law, and I presume it is on account of such that laws are made. Hence, I say that civil liberty, for people living in a state of society, is much better; that is, natural liberty so far abridged and restrained as is necessary and expedient for the safety and interest of the society, state, or nation. I hold that people have a right to do just as they please, provided they do not interfere with the rights of others; but when they do, their liberty, so far, should be stopped.

No man has the liberty, or rather he ought not to have liberty, to deprive another man of *his* liberty, his property, or of any of his personal rights. We have the right, for instance, to stay away from a church on Sunday, if we see fit; but we have no right to forcibly prevent our neighbor from attending such a place if he is so inclined.

As I have said before, there should be no liberty to injure or oppress our fellow-men, for this is wrong, unjust, and tyrannical; when he does this, the public good requires that his liberty be taken from him; because society must, above all earthly considerations, be maintained, particularly as man can subsist only in society, and was by nature adapted for that situation.

All the members of society stand in need of each other's assistance, and are likewise exposed to mutual injuries; but where the necessary assistance is reciprocally afforded from love, from gratitude, from friendship and esteem, the society flourishes and is happy; all the different members of it being bound together by the agreeable bands of love and affection, and are, as it were, drawn to one common center of mutual good offices.

But though the necessary assistance should not be afforded from such generous and disinterested motives, though among the different members of the society there should be no mutual love and affection, the society, though less happy and agreeable, will not necessarily be dissolved, for it may subsist among different men, as among different merchants, from a sense of justice and utility, without any mutual love and affection; and though no man in it should owe any obligation, or be bound in gratitude to any other, it may still be upheld by the laws of necessity—by a mercenary exchange of good offices according to an agreed valuation.

Society, however, can not live among those who are

at all times ready to hurt and injure one another, for the moment that injury begins, the moment that mutual resentment and animosity takes place, all the bands of it are broken asunder, and the different members of which it consisted are, as it were, dissipated and scattered abroad by the violence and opposition of their discordant affections. If there is any society among robbers and murderers, they must, at least, according to the trite observation, abstain from robbing one another. Beneficence, therefore, is less essential to the existence of society than justice, because it may subsist, though not in the most comfortable state, without beneficence; but the prevalence of injustice must utterly destroy it.

Justice, therefore, is the main pillar that upholds the whole edifice, for if it be removed, the great, the immense fabric, which, to raise and support, seems in this world, if I may say so, to have been the peculiar and darling care of nature, must in a moment crumble into atoms.

In order to enforce the observation of justice, therefore, nature has implanted in the human breast that consciousness of ill desert, those dreads of merited punishment which attend upon its violation, as the great safeguards of the association of mankind, to protect the weak, to curb the violent, and to chastise the guilty. Men, though naturally sympathetic, feel so little for another with whom they have no particular connection, in comparison of what they feel for themselves; the misery of one who is merely their fellow-creature is of so little importance to them in comparison even of a small conveniency of their own; they have it so much in their power to hurt him, and may have so many temptations to do so, that if this principle did not stand up within them in his defense and overawe them into a respect for his innocence, they would, like wild beasts, be at all times ready to fly upon him, and a man would enter an assembly of men as he enters a den of lions.

When will the world learn wisdom by the past and hope for the future, and be ashamed and humble when it needs knowledge? Only, I think, when the philosophy of man and mind is developed and admitted as a science by the people generally

In every part of the universe we observe means adjusted with the nicest artifice to the ends which they are intended to produce; and in the mechanism of a plant or animal body, admire how everything is contrived for advancing the two great purposes of nature, the support of the individual and the propagation of the species. But in these, and in all such objects, we still distinguish the efficient from the final cause of their several motions and organizations. The digestion of the food, the circulation of the blood, and the secretion of the several juices which are drawn from it, are operations, all of them necessary for the great purposes of animal life. Yet we never endeavor to account for them from those purposes as from their efficient causes, nor imagine that the blood circulates, or that the food digests of its own accord, and with a view or intention to the purposes of circulation or of digestion. The wheels of the watch are all admirably adjusted to the end for which it was made, the pointing of the hour; and all their various motions conspire in the nicest manner to produce this effect. If they were endowed with a desire and intention to produce it, they could not do it better; yet we never ascribe any such desire or intention to them, but to the watch-maker; and we know that they are put into motion by a spring, which intends the effect it produces as little as they do.

Hence, it is clear that society arises directly from faculties inherited in human nature; and that man can not subsist only in communities, and was by nature fitted for such a condition.

As society can not long exist unless the laws of justice are tolerably observed—as no social intercourse can take place among men who do not generally abstain from injuring one another—the consideration of this necessity, it has been contended, was the ground upon which we approved of the enforcement of the laws of justice, by the punishment of those who violated them. Man has a natural love for society, and desires that the union of mankind should be preserved for its own sake, as though he himself was to derive no benefit from it. The orderly and flourishing state of society is agreeable to him, and he takes delight in contemplating it. Its disorder and confusion, on the contrary, is the object of his aversion, and he is chagrined at whatever tends to produce it. He is sensible, too, that his own interest is connected with the prosperity of the society, and that the happiness, perhaps the preservation of his existence, depends upon its preservation. Upon every account, therefore, he has an abhorrence at whatever tends to destroy society, and is willing to make use of every means which may hinder so hated and so dreadful an event. Injustice necessarily tends to destroy it, and every appearance of injustice, therefore, alarms him, and he runs, if I may say so, to stop the progress of what, if allowed to go on, would quickly put an end to everything that is dear to him. If he can not restrain it by gentle means, he must bear it down by force and violence; at any rate must put a stop to its further progress; and it requires no great discernment to see the destructive tendencies of all licentious practices to the welfare of society, and all men, even the most stupid and unthinking, abhor fraud, perfidy, and injustice, and are ever ready to unite in suppressing everything of the kind. Nevertheless, of one thing I am certain—that we are as yet on the very threshold of knowledge and refinement, and that our social condition is, to a great extent, depravity through and through and from end to end—all for the want of a knowledge of ourselves, of those great laws and principles which underlie and control our actions and affections. But the true philosopher will be all patience for the present and confidence for the future, and never in haste to form institutions in advance of knowledge and the proper condition of society.

CHAPTER III.

OF THE SENSE OF JUSTICE, OF REMORSE, AND OF CONSCIOUSNESS OF MERIT.

"There can be no proper motive for hurting our neighbor; there can be no incitement to do evil to another which mankind will go along with, except just indignation for evil which another has done to us. To disturb his happiness merely because it stands in the way of our own; to take from him what is of real use to him, merely because it may be of equal or more use to us, or to indulge in this manner, at the expense of other people, the natural preference which every man has for his own happiness above that of other people, is what no impartial spectator can go along with.

"Every man is no doubt, by nature, first and principally recommended to his own care; and as he is fitter to take care of himself than of any other person, it is fit and right that it should be so. Every man, therefore, is much more deeply interested in whatever immediately concerns himself than in what concerns any other man; and to hear, perhaps, of the death of another person with whom we have no particular connection will give us less concern, will spoil our stomach, or break our rest, much less than a very insignificant disaster which has befallen ourselves. But though the ruin of our neighbor may affect us much less than a very small misfortune of our own, we must not ruin him to prevent that small misfortune, nor even to prevent our own ruin.

"We must here, as in all other cases, view ourselves, not so much according to that light in which we may naturally appear to ourselves, as according to that in which we naturally appear to others.

"Though every man may, according to the proverb, be the whole world to himself, to the rest of mankind he is a most insignificant part of it

"Though his own happiness may be of more importance to him than that of all the world besides, to every other person it is of no more consequence than that of any other man. Though it may be true, therefore, that every individual in his own breast naturally prefers himself to all mankind, yet he dares not look mankind in the face and avow that he acts according to this principle. He feels that in this preference they can never go along with him, and that how natural soever it may be to him, it must always appear excessive and extravagant to them. When he views himself in the light in which he is conscious that others will view him, he sees that to them he is but one of the multitude, in no respect better than any other in it. If he would so act that the impartial spectator may enter the principles of his conduct, which of all things he has the greatest desire to do, he must upon this, as upon all other occasions, humble the arrogance of his self-love, and bring it down to something which other men can go along with. They will indulge it so far as to allow him to be more anxious about, and to pursue with more earnest assiduity, his own happiness than that of any other person. Thus far, whenever they place themselves in his situation, they will readily go along with him. In the race for wealth, and honors, and preferments, he may run as hard as he can, and strain every nerve and every muscle, in order to outstrip all his competitors. But if he should jostle or throw down any of them, the indulgence of the spectators is entirely at an end. It is a violation of fair play which they can not admit of, because this man is to them in every respect as good as he; they do not enter into that self-love by which he prefers himself so much to this other, and, therefore, can not go along with the motive from which he hurt him.

"They readily, therefore, sympathize with the natural resentment of the injured, and the offender becomes the object of their hatred and indignation. He is sensible that he becomes so, and feels that those sentiments are ready to burst out from all sides against him.

"As the greater and more irreparable the evil that is done, the resentment of the sufferer runs naturally the higher; so does likewise the sympathetic indignation of the spectator, as well as the sense of guilt in the agent. Death is the greatest evil which one man can inflict upon another, and excites the highest degree of resentment in those who are immediately connected with the slain. Murder, therefore, is the most atrocious of all crimes which affect individuals only in the sight of mankind and of the person who has committed it. The most sacred laws of justice, therefore, those whose violation seems to call loudest for resentment and indignation, are the laws which guard the life and person of our neighbor; the next are those which guard his property and possessions; and last of all come those which guard what are called his personal rights, or what is, in short, due to him from the social compact.

"The violator of the more sacred laws of justice can never reflect on the sentiments which mankind must entertain with regard to him, without feeling all the agonies of shame, and horror, and consternation. When his passion is gratified, and he begins coolly to reflect on his past conduct, he can enter into none of the motives which influenced it, because they appear now as detestable to him as they always did to other people. By sympathizing with the hatred and abhorrence which other men must entertain for him, he becomes in some measure the object of his own dislike and abhorrence.

"The situation of the person who suffered by his injustice now calls upon his pity, and he is grieved at the thought of it; regrets the unhappy effects of his own conduct, and the thought of this perpetually haunts him, and fills him with remorse and repentance. He dares no longer look society in the face, but imagines himself, as it were, rejected and thrown out from the affections of all the community; hence he can not hope for the consolation of sympathy in this his greatest distress. Everything seems hostile, and he would be glad to fly to some remote district where he might never more read in the countenance of his acquaintances the condemnation of his crimes.

"Such is the nature of that sentiment properly called

remorse—of all the sentiments which can enter the human mind the most dreadful. It is made up of shame from the sense of the impropriety of past conduct; of grief for the effects of it; of pity for those who suffer by it, and of the dread and terror of punishment from the consciousness of the justly provoked resentment of all rational men. The opposite behavior naturally inspires the opposite sentiment. The man who, not from frivolous fancy, but from proper motives, has performed generous actions, when he looks forward to those whom he has served, feels himself to be the natural object of their love and gratitude, and, by sympathy with them, of the esteem and approbation of all mankind. And when he looks backward to the motive from which he acted, and surveys it in the light in which the indifferent spectator will survey it, he still continues to enter into it, and applauds himself by sympathy with the approbation of this supposed impartial judge. In both of these points of view, his own conduct appears to him every way agreeable. His mind, at the thought of it, is filled with cheerfulness, serenity, and composure. He is in friendship and harmony with all mankind, and looks upon his fellow-citizens with confidence and benevolent satisfaction, confident that he has rendered himself worthy of their most favorable regards.

"In the combination of all these sentiments consists the consciousness of *merit*, or of deserved respect."— *Smith's T. of M. Sentiments.*

"A wise man will hear, and will increase learning; and a man of understanding shall attain unto wise counsels."—*Proverbs:* 5.

CHAPTER IV.

PHILOSOPHY.

WHAT is philosophy? It is the observation of effects in relation to causes, in order to the discovery of the laws concerned, and consists practically in the knowledge of and in the application of general truth.

What should be the highest object of philosophers? It should be to attain to that state of intelligence and refinement in which they may be enabled to harmonize the opposing forces and conflicting elements; to extract good, *present* or *future*, from all doctrines, theories, and circumstances; to appreciate and enjoy all things; recognizing the true value and relations of every character, condition, and circumstance; their knowledge being so full, and their enjoyments so high, that they may regret but very little through life—a truly enlightened and noble mind would not be subject to grief.

Yes, the highest and greatest end of philosophy, both natural and moral, should be to know and to bless ourselves and our kind; and the highest learning is to be wise, and the greatest wisdom is to be good.

Socrates, who made all his philosophy subservient to morality, took more pains to rectify the habits and tempers of his pupils, than to replenish their understanding, and regarded all knowledge as useless speculation that was not brought to this end, to make us wiser and better men, and hence more useful citizens.

It was a very just and sensible answer which Agesilaus, the Spartan king, returned to one who asked him, "What it was in which youth ought principally to be instructed? He replied, "That which they have most need to practice when they are men." Were this single rule but carefully attended to in the method of education, it might probably be conducted in a manner much more to the advantage of our youth than it now is, for the pains we take in books or arts, which treat of things remote from the use of life, is but a busy idleness. And what is there in life which youth will have more frequent occasion to practice than the proper cultivation and government of their appetites, passions, and prejudices? What is there in which they need more direction and assistance? What is there which they afterward more regret the want of?

Or what better reason to receive that assistance and to lay a foundation for this difficult, but very important science, than the early part of youth?

It may be said that it is properly the office and the care of parents to watch over and correct the tempers and habits of their children in the first years of their infancy, when it may be easiest done; but if it be not done effectually then (as it very seldom is), there is the more necessity for it afterward.

But the truth is, it is the proper office and care of all who have the charge of children, and ought to be looked upon as the most important and necessary part of education, for he who acquires his learning at the expense of his morals is the worse for his education. And I may add that he who does not improve his moral and social habits together with his understanding, is not much the better for it; because he ought to measure his progress in science by the improvement of his morals and usefulness, remembering that he is no further a learned man than he is a wise, useful, and good one.

CHAPTER V.

NATURE AND NATURE'S WORKS.

The inscription upon the temple of Isis, the personification of the great mother, nature, was: "I am whatsoever is, whatsoever has been, whatsoever shall be."

Life and death follow in unceasing vicissitude; winter prepares the earth for the genial influence of spring; the vernal warmth causes trees and plants to disclose their blossoms, which summer develops into fruit; the sea supplies, through the air, the rivers with their perennial streams; they return their waters to the deep, and thus all things perpetually revolve in an undeviating round. The world exists but by conflict, and is only maintained by opposition. Combat is the key to all nature's grand successes. All things find their contrarieties to be the foundation of their preservation and their perpetuity. We ever find one force pitted against another. Within our own bodies is the contest fiercely waged a few short years, till the assailants gain the ascendency, when the citadel falls. All the changes which happen in nature serve but for its duration; for while everything tends to its end, nature exists the same—is permanent. The same things always compose it, and one, interminating, only supplies room for others to succeed it; the end of the first forms the commencement of the second; and while all things are perishable, it is that succession may take place—that mankind may be preserved, and the earth's consistency be confirmed. Mutability may be said to constitute the harmony of the universe.

Nature, in whatever point of view we consider it, can not possibly be anything but that which we perceive it to be. It is whatsoever is, whatsoever has been, whatsoever shall be. The ancients entertained no fearful ideas respecting death, because observing faithfully the course of nature, they knew all things were finite and terminate in destruction, in order that life may be transmitted to a succession of beings.

The series of natural forms and combinations is eternal, but all particular beings of this eternal series are transitory.

The infinite orders of existence operate by affinities for each other, so that the infinite chain of being is connected together by infinite links of relation; and the farther we venture in the wide field of analysis, the more we discover that we lose our pains in searching after any other element or basis which may be considered a primary principle of existence. It is by virtue of the nutritive action or nutrition that the organs of the body preserve or change their physical properties, and the changes in the moral being correspond. What physiologists have called the "vital force," is but the necessary or natural exercise of the functions which animal organization possesses, and which exertion is compelled by calls of animal affinities or wants, the gratification of which exigencies are indispensable to its existence, particularly that of nutrition. Art may trace the action of those minute portions of matter called seeds or ova, known to the rudiments of future life, and the links by which the chain of endless generation hang to existence; but the eternal principle can never be disentangled and displayed apart—that principle, under the influence of which each little gem, in due time, swells out as if to fill an invisible mold of maturity that determines its form and proportions—that function by which the animal body assumes foreign matters from abroad and converts them into its own substance.

In the economy of life it is a general law that living beings derive their origin from similar pre-existing beings, like following like; the vital motions of animation are communicated from the parent stock; it is life that gives origin to life.

The striking characteristics of animated beings are generation and death. Life is motion superinduced in matter peculiarly arranged, and death is the cessation of this motion.

Vital principle, or principle of life, are the terms used to denote the phenomena of animation. Organization, which is the primary condition of life, necessarily precedes the action of those organs, in the exercise of which consists the functions of life. The action of every organ constitutes what is called its functions. Without the organ there is no function, for the plain reason that without the instrument by which the action is produced there is no action—without the instrument there is no music.

It is to nature, animate and inanimate, that we must look for all our information and improvements—for all our earthly blessings; because her habitudes and laws furnish all our science, and, indeed, all the models of our art. She is all that is within our reach or the uttermost stretch of our research. If we dig into the earth, among minerals, soils, fountains, and eternal fires, there we find only her habitations and her works; if we examine the atmosphere, the electric fluid, the gentle ripple of the brook, they all tell us only of nature. If we look into the flowers, examine the fruits, dissect the most minute structure of plants and animals, observe their modes of life, their passions, their wants, their joys, their sorrows, their hopes, their fears, the gentle kiss of love, or the fierce collisions of war; whether they burst into new life, or decay and sleep again in the earth; whether there be the ringing laugh of joyous youth, or the solemn repose of death; whether we direct our attention to this earth and its productions, or point the eye of the telescope to other planets and other stars and other groups of suns, far off into the immeasurable distance—all, all is vast universal nature, and science is its interpretation.

Therefore, all that we should attempt, and all that is possible for us to do, is to view things on earth as they are or seem to be, and having done this much to some extent, will next contemplate the works of nature in relation to the beauties and wonders of the planetary worlds.

There are but few who have had the benefit of instruction, probably few who are sensible of existence, that have not raised their eyes in a cloudless night to the starry firmament, and who have not felt some emotion, however undefined, at what they see there.

Familiar as this continually-recurring spectacle may be, it is ever magnificent and ever new, and ever fills the mind with astonishment and awe.

Examined by the light of science and contemplated in its systematic regularity, the feelings of astonishment and awe sink deeper and deeper, and though I am not prepared to say that "an undevout astronomer is mad," I can imagine that he must be a very peculiar man if this science does not fill his mind with admiration of the wonders of nature and of his capacity to comprehend them.

For really it is wonderful that such a transient and comparatively insignificant being as he who moves on the surface of this little globe, and who is tied down to it by the irresistible power of attraction, should be able to foretell with unerring certainty the very moment when the light of the sun will be shut out from the earth by the intervening of its satellite.

Nay, the precise moment when a comet was visible from our little globe, at a time long past, when he was not in being himself, and when it will again be visible when he must be gone, and perhaps unremembered on earth.

Astronomers tell us also that the sun is 520 times larger than all the planetary globes which revolve around him, and 1,300,000 times larger than our own globe. Such is the power of this luminary that the planet Herschel is held in its orbit, lighted, and warmed by his brilliancy, at the distance of 1,800,000,000 of miles from his surface.

Besides the sun and the planets which revolve around him, there belongs to the same system comets, the purpose of which is apparently inconceivable. Their magnitude and rapidity of motion are equally so. They, too, are nevertheless known to insignificant mortals to move with exact precision.

One of them is, by human agency, known to be 11,200,000,000 of miles from the sun at its greatest distance, and to move at the rate of 880,000 miles in an hour when nearest to him. The tail of the comet which appeared in 1680 was computed by Sir Isaac Newton to be 80,000,000 of miles in length.

Magnificent and glorious as the solar system may be, what is it in magnitude and distance when compared with the innumerable worlds, the systems upon systems of worlds, yea, the seas upon seas of worlds still beyond it; and yet how noiselessly, how harmoniously, do they all move around an unknown parental center. Indeed, infinity seems wreathed with worlds, and every one decorated with lesser worlds, like mighty flowers of unutterable grandeur, all flying through the boundless realms of infinite space with a speed inconceivable, and causing not so much sound as the ticking watch; all inhabited with multiplied millions of human beings, some perhaps inferior to us, while the greater part are, no doubt, far superior in all human attributes and acquirements.

Astronomy demonstrates the being and attributes of God, the source of all sublimity, and exhibits the most striking proofs of his wisdom, his power, and his goodness. It develops those eternal laws by which he keeps in order and harmony the vast and complicated movements of millions of inhabited worlds.

> The spacious firmament on high,
> With all the blue ethereal sky,
> And spangled heavens, a shining frame,
> Their great original proclaim.
> The unwearied sun, from day to day,
> Does his Creator's power display;
> And publishes to every land,
> The work of an Almighty hand.
> Soon as the evening shades prevail,
> The moon takes up the wond'rous tale;
> And nightly, too, the list'ning earth
> Repeats the story of her birth;
> Whilst all the stars that round her burn,
> And all the planets in their turn,
> Confirm the tidings as they roll,
> And spread the truth from pole to pole.
> What though in solemn silence all,
> Move 'round this dark terrestrial ball;
> What though no real voice nor sound
> Amidst their radiant orbs be found;
> In reason's ear they all rejoice,
> And utter forth a glorious voice;
> For ever singing as they shine:
> The Hand that made us is divine.

In every clear night the naked eye may discover nearly a thousand fixed stars, which are supposed to be luminaries as the sun. If all these luminaries are suns, and have their attendant planets, as we know our sun to have, it would comprise a mass of matter equal to 132,000,000 of globes the size of our earth. The assistance which the human eye has obtained in extending its views into nature's works, by artificial means, discloses to us the certainty that orbs exist at such a distance from us, that a common ball, moving at the rate of 480 miles an hour, would require 9,000,000 of years to pass from some of them to the earth. The sun is computed to be 95,000,000 of miles from the earth; yet in eight minutes and a quarter the light reaches the earth from that luminary. What must be the magnitude of luminous bodies, which are seen with the help of glasses at such a distance that it would require some years for light to come from them to the earth? From whatever point on the surface of our sphere the eye is directed toward the firmament, worlds on worlds, systems on systems, are disclosed. Where shall the imagination fix the boundaries of creation? Are we in the center of the universe, or are we in some remote extremity? What is the center, and what is an extremity of the universe? If there be a center, and if there be limits to nature's works, what is there beyond them, and who and what exists where nature does not exist and reign?

But if we are astonished at the magnitude and distance of these luminaries, how much more so must we be when we try to think of them collectively and in motion? We know that, like the substances on the earth, they are held by the law of gravitation, and we know what strength it requires to move a weight of a few hundred pounds. If we could suppose our comparatively small earth to be a perfectly smooth ball on a plane, it is believed that it would require a mechanical force which no human mind can compute to give it any motion. Yet we know it moves at the rate of 68,000 miles in every hour, revolving as it flies; and that that motion which causes day and night is its rotation on its axis; and that which makes a period of time called a year, is likewise known to be its revolution around the sun. Now, if the circumference of the globe be somewhere about 25,000, and its annual course 60,000,000 of miles, it must follow that everybody living on the equator is turned around in twenty hours 25,000 miles, and all are moved forward through space during the same twenty-four hours the astonishing distance of above 1,600,000 miles!

Such are some of natures's physical works; and though no person of knowledge doubts the fact, yet no person, learned or ignorant, ever feels the motion in the slightest degree!

This remarkable instance of the wonderful mechanism of *nature*, of which we form a part, may be expected, when clearly exposed, to make us extremely cautious in drawing our conclusions concerning the moral operations of nature's works, merely from our various sensations.

The foregoing reflections arose from the observation of the actual state of the human species over the surface of the earth, and from a consideration of the prevailing sentiment by which all the different societies of men are governed, and their actions judged; and will it be possible that any one, when thus led to reflect, shall remain blind to the error of such a sentiment after so many years of continued misery?

Shall our deceitful sensations still misguide our judgment, and shall mankind forever believe that they are the intentional authors of their own misfortunes? Shall not the history of kingdoms upon kingdoms at length undeceive them? Shall they go on, from generation to generation, holding the opinion that they can make themselves, intellectually, morally, and socially, almost entirely independent of natural influences—that men are free agents and can do just as they see fit, while they are everywhere guided and governed by the progressive changes of nature, by the knowledge which her operations bring to light, and by the circumstances which she, in this manner and by her own power, places them in. Nature physically moves man, while he is quite unconscious of the motion; and mentally moves him, though there are, unfortunately, but very few who are sufficiently acquainted with her laws in relation to themselves to *know* the great truth.

CHAPTER VI.

SOCIAL REFORM—CIRCUMSTANCES.

This is a very important subject, and to investigate it properly requires considerable knowledge of those laws and influences which govern and control human nature.

For many years I have entertained the opinion that men are what they are according to their entailments and the circumstances which surround them in after life, and I know not how else to account for the differences in their physical, moral, and social conditions.

Nobody, I presume, in this world, ever desired to be sickly, poor, and unhappy, having literally "a hard time of it" all through life; yet there are thousands upon thousands thus placed. Now if they did not desire this condition, how came they in it? This is the question. If the universal desire is for happiness and not misery, how comes it about that there is so little of the former and so much of the latter.

Again, I say, this is the question, and I wish I knew how to make unalloyed happiness the general rule and misery the exception. The Christian will tell us that human nature is wicked—prone to evil as the sparks fly upward; and some specimens of human nature that I have seen were very bad, it must be confessed; but that even they actually wanted to be so is very improbable. Natural wickedness, therefore, is not the cause. What is? I may not be able to give a satisfactory answer, but I have an idea that if one word more than another contains the answer, it is to be found in the word "*circumstances.*" A long word—and so it should be, if its character can thus be measured, for wrapped up in it are the causes of war, slavery, intemperance, bigotry, and the rest of the catalogue of national and social troubles.

But to come more particularly to the subject, and to answer an inquiry which might arise in the minds of some of my readers, what do you mean by a circumstance? Everything which in any way operates upon or influences man is a circumstance. Men perform no action without a motive of some kind; and all their motives to thought and to exertion arise, either immediately or remotely, from the operation of surrounding circumstances upon them. If deprived of food, men become hungry; if of drink, thirsty; if disappointed in their expectations and thwarted in their desires, they are discontented and unhappy.

All these feelings or sensations are the effects of particular circumstances upon sentient organization; they can not be destroyed by any mere effort of thinking or willing, and thus they become the causes of motives and the inciters to action. From the nature of man, therefore, he must ever be the creature of circumstances; he will ever passively receive impressions from surrounding objects; for he can not, by taking thought, alter his organization, or add one cubit to his stature.

Now, in respect to character, man has a capacity to

be almost anything, and by turns almost everything, as circumstances shall determine. He, like the floating bubble on the stream, shows us, at times, many colors and mixtures of colors; but these various shades of character, however light or dark, are little more than reflex radiations from surrounding objects and occurrences. The simple nature of man is colorless; it is fitted to receive every variety of impressions; and, when the combined nature and impression call forth an action, good or bad, such action discloses not so much the hue of the nature itself, as the hue which it has taken from the bright or the gloomy influences to which it has been exposed. If, then, we would have the family of man to be, as it were, a bright and glorious assemblage of the pictures of humanity, we must place all men in positions and surround them with circumstances and influences in which there shall be nothing (if possible) black and unseemly.

It matters not what may be the mere knowledge given to men, or the moral and religious precepts taught, if the other circumstances by which they are surrounded be disregarded. Bad circumstances and influences can neither produce nor maintain good men. Circumstances furnish the seed of good or ill, and man is but the soil in which they grow. The characters of men may be made entirely good or quite bad; but if the institutional crcumstances and influences which surround them do not accord with the end desired—do not contain within them more of good than of evil—then that which was intended to be a beautiful garden will become either choked up by noxious weeds, or converted into a blighted or barren waste.

All these considerations respecting the nature of man, and the influences of surrounding circumstances upon that nature, plainly show that the present habits and prejudices of the various classes of society, and their feelings of reverence or contempt toward each other, result from the social position of one class with respect to another, and the difference of the circumstances by which each class is surrounded; and, therefore, it necessarily follows—what has been proved by universal experience—that were the position and circumstances of each class reversed, the characters of each would be changed, and the crawling slave of to-day would become the domineering tyrant of to-morrow. All men are of one substance and one nature; they are made into tyrants and slaves—into ignorant, dissipated, wicked, deceitful, and dishonest citizens—by the present social system, by land monopoly, and the consequent division of society into rich and poor; and this division is maintained, not because the first class is superior to the latter in mental and corporeal attributes, but because the two exchange unequally with each other.

History shows us how little has been the success of man in controlling the various circumstances which have relation to his existence and his happiness.

Woefully has he sinned and suffered. He has blindly destroyed the wealth and shed the blood of his fellow-man, simply because his fellow-man felt and thought just the same as he himself would have felt and thought, had he been placed in the same position and exposed to the same influences. The tyranny and wrong at any time to be removed is not in the men, but in the institutions; and wherever a physical revolution has overturned a governmental despotism, and left untouched the social institutions from which that despotism sprang, it has never led, and never can lead, to any other result than a transfer of power from one man or one class of men to another; for the last are left exposed to the same influences as the first, and therefore they necessarily revive the apparently subverted tyranny. The empire of love can be extended from families and friends to nations and the world at large only by uprooting those social institutions which circumscribe the love of man to man within the narrow circle of a class.

CHAPTER VII.

THOUGHTS ON PREJUDICE.

All men imagine that on this globe there is no part of it, in this part of the earth no nation, in the nation no province, in the province no city, in the city no society, comparable to their own. We, step by step, surprise ourselves into a secret persuasion that we are superior to all our acquaintances. If an oyster, confined in its shell, is acquainted with no more of the universe than the rock on which it is fixed, and therefore can not judge of its extent, how can a man in the midst of a small society, always surrounded by the same objects and acquainted with only one train of thoughts, be able to form a proper estimate of the different societies and peoples without his own circle? Truth is never engendered or perceived but in the fermentation of contrary opinions. The universe is only known to us in proportion as we become acquainted with it, and whoever confines himself to conversing with only one set of companions can not avoid adopting their prejudices, especially if they flatter his pride. Who can separate himself from an error when vanity and prejudice, the companions of ignorance, have tied him to it and rendered it dear unto him?

We need more toleration of individual opinions, more liberality, and less prejudice. There must be a certain conformity to laws and social regulations, of course, and whatever may be necessary to the safety and good order of society, every one should cheerfully submit to; but why need we go beyond this? If people differ in opinion, or in taste, or in personal habits, or in the color of their hair, or in the length and shape of their noses, it need not be a cause of enmity and persecution. We must not be guilty of dissipation, or pick our neighbor's pockets; but our believing in one or two more or less articles in our creed should not worry and alienate him.

In practical morals we must, of course, agree; but is it any matter what theories we hold on purely speculative subjects?

People who attend two churches in the same village hold diametrically opposite opinions upon some question of morals and religion, but so long as they can agree to respect and tolerate each other's opinions, no great harm is done. They can get bread of the same baker, and trade at the same grocery; but let their notions be carried into religion or politics, and very soon, perhaps, war is begun. As a people, we boast of our liberality and toleration in matters of thought and of conscience, but it is very doubtful whether we have the right to make such a boast, for it appears to me that our prejudices and hatreds have grown more and more violent. Honest men of one belief proscribe and denounce equally useful and conscientious men of another.

Toleration is almost forgotten. Press and pulpit, the rostrum of the lecturer and the stump of the political debater, are *intemperately* arrayed against each other, all for the want of a better knowledge of *ourselves*, and of the laws and principles necessary to govern a community—all for the want of a proper acquaintance with those great laws and influences which underlie and control our notions, actions, and affections, which govern men mentally, morally, and socially.

Indeed, such is the universal ignorance of the people in relation to the above-named laws and influences, that there are more than nineteen-twentieths of them who do not really know how to live, under many circumstances, practical, moral, or religious men and women.

From the fact a man can no more live rightly without knowing how, than he can make a wagon or violin without knowing how, and the former a thousand times more difficult to learn than the latter; hence so much wrangling, persecution, condemnation, and vengeance in every community for mere imaginary wrongs. Therefore, we should all learn to

BE CHARITABLE.

"Do not rashly judge your brother,
If he stumbles in the way;
Life's beset with sore temptation,
He has fallen—and we may.

"Let us rather kindly help him
To regain the pathway lost;
Gentle words are never wasted,
Freely *give*—they *little* cost.

"Take good heed unto thy footsteps,
Round the walks lurks many a snare,
If like him shouldst be tempted,
Oh, *my brother, watch, beware!*

> "For we grope our way so blindly
> Through the darksome shades of life,
> And the best will err so often
> 'Mid its tumult, toil, and strife."

It is the philosopher alone who contemplates the manners, laws, customs, religions, and the different appetites and passions that actuate mankind; who can become almost insensible both to the praise and satire of the people; can break all the chains of prejudice; examine with modesty and indifference the various opinions which divide the human family; pass without astonishment from a seraglio to a cloister; reflect with serenity on the extent of human folly—who knows that our ideas necessarily proceed from the company we keep, the books we read, and the objects presented to our sight, and that a superior intelligence might divine our thoughts from the objects presented before us, and from our thoughts divine the number and nature of the objects offered to the mind.

The Arab, persuaded of the infallibility of his Khaliff, laughs at the credulity of the Tartar, who firmly believes the great Lama immortal. The negro in Africa, who pays his adorations to the claw of a lobster or the horn of an animal, sees nothing on the earth but myriads of deities, and laughs at the scarcity of gods among us, while the ill-informed Musselman accuses us of acknowledging three.

If a sage should descend from heaven and in his language and conduct consult only the lights of instinct and reason, he would most likely pass for a fool. Mankind are so scrupulously attached to the interest of their own prejudice and vanity, that the title of wise is only given to the fools of the common folly. The more foolish an opinion is, the more dangerous it is to prove its folly. Fontenelle was accustomed to say that if he held every truth in his hand, he would take great care not to open it to show them to men.

In destroying prejudices, we ought to treat them with respect. Like the doves from the ark, we ought to send some truths on the discovery to see if the deluge of prejudices does not yet cover the face of the earth, if error begins to subside, and if there can be perceived here and there some isles where wisdom and truth may find rest for their feet and communicate themselves to mankind.

All those customs originate from the education and prejudices of the people, the observance of which can not, as it seems to me, contribute much to the public happiness, such as the austerities of the senseless Fakirs with which the Indias are peopled.

These idle customs in most nations (for many of them are to be found in every nation under heaven) are more honored than the genuine virtues, and those who practice them held in greater veneration than good citizens.

Happy the people among whom the customs which originate from prejudice and folly are only ridiculed—they are frequently extremely barbarous.

In the capital of Cochin they bring up crocodiles, and whoever exposes himself to the fury of one of these monsters and is devoured, is reckoned among the elect; and what is more barbarous than the institution of convents among the Papists? As there are virtues of prejudice, there are also vices of prejudices.

The neglect in Catholic countries of fasts, confessions, penances, etc., is a crime of the first magnitude.

And there is perhaps no country where the people have so great an abhorrence of the violation of these customs of prejudice—a greater abhorrence than they have for villainies the most atrocious and the most injurious to society.

Such are some of the follies and baneful consequences of *prejudice*—the child of ignorance.

But we of the nineteenth century, who boast so much of our civilization and liberality, should cherish their virtues, and from their follies learn to

"Seize upon truth wherever found,
On Christian or on heathen ground;
Among our friends, among our foes,
The plant's divine where'er it grows.'

CHAPTER VIII.

A SKETCH OF NATURAL HISTORY.

ALL the natural objects that surround us are the subjects of natural history, and much of the improvements and enjoyments of civilized life are founded on our knowledge of animals, vegetables, minerals, and fluids.

The endless variety of subjects it embraces, and the peaceful nature of the pursuit, render this study not less interesting and agreeable than it is useful. Every animal or insect that presents itself, a few plants which may be gathered anywhere, a shell or a pebble that may be picked up on the roadside, or on the sea-shore, suffice to afford the naturalist subjects of reflection and an ample fund of intellectual enjoyment.

Natural history is becoming an important part of education; and the soft rising beams of its morning are silently and steadily creeping into the nooks and corners, dispelling the dark mists of bigotry, superstition, and error, and leaving light and loveliness in their room.

When this knowledge, embracing as it does, the great laws of entailment and of mind—those principles, agencies and influences which underlie and control all the actions and affections of men—shall have been spread broadly over all parts of society, then the rotten props of old-established follies will tumble to the earth, and the dens and strongholds of ignorance and mysticism will be cleared away with those masses of filth and nonsense which ages have been piling together.

Now the first fact that strikes us, when looking at the animal kingdom, is the exact order which prevails throughout animated being. Every family of this kingdom has its peculiar place assigned to it; to that place it is perfectly adapted, and to none other. In that appropriate sphere it comes into being, finds its own share in the physical, mental, and social world; in that it continues, and in that expires. All its instincts, propensities, faculties, pleasures, aversions, enmities, and wars have their own peculiar objects.

For each of these innumerable classes, from the elephant to the smallest mite that the microscope discloses to us on the dried fruit or the purest lily's leaf, and in the transparent drop of spring water, there are laws of being far more definite, and far more faithfully obeyed, than any which proud intellectual man can make and enforce.

That life is a blessing, and intended to be so understood and enjoyed, is proven by the sense which every living thing seems instinctively to have of its value; and the endless diversity which is found in preserving and continuing life is among the striking proofs of the power and uniformity of natural law. And is it not surprising that among the thousands of varieties, which have been distinctly enumerated and classed by zoologists, amounting to not less than one hundred and fifty thousand—say one thousand species of mammalia, six thousand of birds, two thousand of reptiles, and one hundred and twenty thousand species of insects —as belonging to the earth and its waters, mingled together as they seem to the human eye, that every species appears to know and preserve its place, and each one to keep distinct from all others from age to age? What is it that preserves each one, and prevents the confusion, which would bring on, in a very short succession, one common ruin?

There are some general laws which seem to be common to all animal existence, and among them the necessity of food. From this fact it is certain that all animated nature is subject to daily waste which demands a daily supply; and this demand appears to be intended to be satisfied in part from the vegetable creation, and in part from the fitness of some animals to furnish food for others. By this law, the animal kingdom seems to be going through a successive change, by which animals of one kind become parts of others; and the vegetable world makes the like contribution to animal life, and the latter again makes its contribution to the common mother of all, which, in the course of exercising its functions, sends forth its preparation for the same revolutionary course. Certainly in all this there is abundant proof to every contemplative mind of natural law undeviatingly pursued.

But it has been objected that it is inconsistent with the benevolence of nature that some animated beings are necessary to others as food. A moment's reflection, however, will show that this objection can not be sustained consistently with obvious laws; for if some sorts of animals did not prey upon others, the common food must be vegetable; and suppose all animals and insects were left to increase in numbers, as we know they would do, and that all were to find food from vegetable products, how long would it probably be before all of them perish for want of food? Supposing existence a benefit, and considering the numbers that escape destruction, it will be found that this provision so complained of is consistent with general laws, and consequently with the benevolence of nature. In the ocean, if the same law as to food did not prevail, its inhabitants would soon come to an end, for it is known that one fish may produce millions of fish. Now if the increase were permitted according to this scale, and some fish were not consumed by others, it seems that the whole would perish for want of food. But the God of Nature has wisely and mercifully provided against such a fatal necessity, by creating, as it were, certain police over nearly every family of animated being, in order to so regulate the increase that none should die of starvation. For instance, the owl, hawk, mink, etc., are the police over the bird kind, and often over the feathered tribes, small animals; the cat kind over the ox, sheep, deer, goat, etc.; the large fish over the smaller ones. But it was left for man to provide his own police, which he never fails to do in the shape of war.

Again, it is known that variety and peculiarity is one of nature's fundamental and all-prevading laws; and which was, in part, necessary to manifest her infinite wisdom and goodness—necessary for the edification and gratification of all the people of the earth; but which could not have been so illimitably extended, as we now find it, without such a provision—without some sorts of animals could subsist upon others. Now if we descend from these very general views to some particulars, we shall see new proofs of this theory. The sagacity with which some animals are gifted is truly wonderful; and the natural history of the spider may be referred to for this. The migration of certain birds is another proof. Certain birds and quadrupeds have a kind of knowledge to which even man is a stranger.

Pigeons and some domestic animals, when carried miles from their homes, in covered conveyances, have a power of discerning the way back; and the common bee knows the straight line to its hive at all times, however far it may have wandered, and however often it may have crossed its own track. The senses of birds and animals appear to have been given to them for the spheres in which they live and move, and in which they are to wage war, fly from danger, or secure their food. Those who are curious in natural history will find abundant means of gratification in examining the works of the universe; and the more minute the research is, the more will it serve to convince the mind that nature is fixed and eternal in the inherent laws by which she is governed. This, I venture to assert, is a conviction from which the human mind can not escape.

CHAPTER IX.

CAUSES OF CRIME AND TREATMENT OF CRIMINALS.

The causes of crime are various and numerous, yet they originate not in the people themselves, but from their surrounding circumstances. Bad circumstances and influences can neither produce nor maintain good men.

Circumstances furnish the seed of good or evil, and man is but the soil in which they grow. As well blame the soil for growing the thistle after we had sowed the seed.

All men are of one substance and of one nature; they are made into tyrants and slaves, into dissipated, deceitful, dishonest, and wicked citizens, by our present social system; for by land monopoly we create tyrants and slaves, war and polygamy; also, rob and starve the millions; thereby indirectly seducing and forcing them into theft and robbery in order to live. And with our votes charter certain houses and license certain men, " of good character," to deal out to our well-meaning but imprudent citizens the liquid poison which fires their blood, debases their morals, dethrones their reason, and hence induces very many of them to violate the laws in every possible manner.

Therefore, it is obvious that our crimes proceed only

from our education, mal-legislation, and the pernicious entailments too often fastened on us; and which entailments proceed from the past indulgence of our ancestry in dissipation and crime, or from their incompatible alliances—the fact being obvious, that we entail on our progeny, more or less, not only our sinful habits, but our every thought, talent, appetite, passion, and disease—like following like.

Hence, how vastly important it is that all persons who are instrumental in imparting life should live strictly in obedience to the requirements of good morals and true religion; not even allowing themselves to indulge, for a moment, an evil thought.

Yes, it is from an imperfect, false, and vicious education—from ignorance—that all our mal-legislation, poverty, misery, and crime proceed. It is from *ignorance*, because every man loves himself well enough to desire liberty, self-preservation, and happiness, and would, by the forces of nature, promote the same were he only sufficiently enlightened; he is not an oyster or an owl; hence requires liberty and light. It is the ignorance of his own true and best interests—of his moral, social, and political rights—which causes him to transgress the laws of life, of humanity, and of society.

In other words, it is the want of a true education—by which is meant a full and harmonious development of all his powers and faculties—and a good knoweldge of the practical duties of life; a knowledge of himself, of the great laws of mind, and his relations to other men, to society, and to the external world. Then, and not until then, can he ever know how to be a good and law-abiding citizen—how to treat himself and other men under all the various circumstances through life.

Another great cause of crime is, that tens of thousands of well-meaning parents, owing to a false affection for their children, indulge them in impudence, disobedience, idleness, and extravagance; teaching them to believe that about all they need in this world is plenty of fine apparel and a little book education, ignoring about all the essential knowledge pertaining to the laws of their own being and of a useful and practical life. And. through a vain and foolish pride are ashamed to give them a useful trade or business in order that they might live honestly by their labor; indeed, a good proportion of our criminals are men, "gentlemen," who are brought up without any productive business, and who, being reduced to want, feel constrained to steal or rob to live.

Again, society has become so vain and reckless that moral principle or moral honesty is almost lost sight of by vast numbers—whatever happens to be popular or available being all right; indeed, even the various organizations are but too successfully sought as masks and protection from crime.

Another great cause of crime may be found (as before mentioned) in our thousands and tens of thousands of whisky saloons, which our unwise but honest voters have established all over our country, and at almost every man's door; there to seduce themselves and their sons into habits of folly, idleness, and dissipation. And our free use of tobacco is a powerful auxiliary to this gigantic system of degeneracy, demoralization, and crime; from the fact this tobacco is a narcotic substance which stupefies the brain and depresses the heart's action, consequently strongly predisposing its subjects to alcoholic drinks in order to counteract the aforesaid depressing and stupefying effects. Hence it is certain that our general and excessive use of this narcotic produces more than the one-third of all the inebriates of our general country—the one-third of all our poverty, dissipation, and wretchedness; and crimes, endless crimes, are their natural and constant companions. And, strange to tell! our better class of citizens, including a large proportion of our "gentlemen," are to blame for nearly all this crime, misery, and degradation by their setting the hateful and seductive examples to our boys, not only in the use of the "nasty weed," but patronizing the retreats of iniquity. When will men cease to be children?

But the chief and fundamental cause of crime originates from land monopoly, which is, and ever was, the prolific source of all those excesses of ignorance, servility, and crime found among men. It circumscribes the advantages and privileges of the many—of millions. It concentrates too much the wealth and resources of our general country into the hands, comparatively speaking, of individuals, and thereby deprives them of their natural right to a fair share of the soil which is not the product of man, but the gift of God to all his children without respect to any. It allows the rich, by mal-legislation, to oppress the poor in every possible manner, denying them, virtually, the right to humble domiciles, and to the thousands of other common gifts and benefits of mother earth.

Hence they are perpetuated in poverty, ignorance, and degradation, which, taken together (as we too often find them) is, and ever has been, a fruitful source of crime.

Then, with all the foregoing before us, can we wonder that so many criminals excuse themselves for their transgressions of the laws? Then is it any wonder that we have so much poverty, dissipation, and crime in every community? Is it any wonder that our asylums and prisons are ever filled with the unhappy victims of pernicious laws, education, and entailment—with the victims of dissipation and crime. I only wonder that we have not far more poverty, ignorance, and crime than we now have. I only wonder and rejoice that my race is capable of so much forbearance, resignation, fortitude, and virtue under so many gross wrongs and abuses.

Then let us next consider, in humanity, how we, as an enlightened and christian people, should treat these criminals.

The treatment of criminals is one of the most difficult and important subjects that ever engaged the minds of philanthropists and statesmen. Upon the solution of this problem depends the hopes for the restoration of criminals and of moral character in the young who manifest an incipient proclivity to crime. The principles upon which this renovation should proceed are clearly indicated by the structure and laws of the brain.

As regards the young, it is, in the first place, essential

that the moral organs should be kept in vigorous and sustained activity, until, by systematic cultivation and growth, they acquire a perfectly controlling power.

Secondly, it is necessary that the over-active animal organs should be gradually checked and restrained, until they become entirely subordinate to the higher powers.

Thirdly, it is necessary that the animal organs should be trained to act in co-operation with the intellectual and moral, and thus acquiring a legitimate sphere of activity, should be enabled to attain that development which is necessary to the perfection of the whole constitution.

These measures have never been conjoined and efficiently carried out in the systematic manner requisite for the restoration of depraved characters, either young or old, in the schools or in the prisons. I believe we may reasonably expect from the efficient and systematic application of these principles a radical change and moral regeneration in a large majority of the depraved characters to whom they are applied. The necessity of intellectual and moral education is well known, but this principle is not acted upon in our public prisons (or moral murder pens) as it should be. A well-educated man is rarely found in the state prison, and one would suppose that a government, aware of "the incompatibility of moral and intellectual culture and low crime, would endeavor to give to all unfortunate people who have fallen into criminal habits that education, which, had it been given to them sooner, would have prevented their vices and crimes.

But I would not have our criminals educated in our present penitentiaries any longer than until state governments could have time to erect, for purely reformatory purposes, new and appropriate edifices.

Ever since civilization commenced, society has been experimenting to discover the requisite punishments for crimes, and yet the discovery has to be made. We must conclude that is a strange fact, when we reflect that every variety and extreme of punishment has been tried, and all have failed, and that as civilization is extended and advanced, crime increases.

But punishment is no longer considered, except by the ignorant and sanguinary, as vengeance from the injured, or expiation from the guilty. We now distinctly understand that the greatest possible happiness of the whole society must be the ultimate object of all just legislation; that the partial evil of punishment is consequently to be tolerated by the wise and humane legislator only so far as it is proven to be necessary for the general good.

When a crime has been committed, it can not be undone by all the art or all the power of man; by vengeance the most sanguinary, or remorse the most painful.

The fact is irrevocable; all that remains is to provide for the future. It would be absurd, after an offense has already been committed, to increase the sum of misery in the world by inflicting pain upon the offender; because he murdered my brother that is no reason that I should murder him; because he stole my horse that is no reason why I should steal his horse; because two wrongs can not make a right.

But by the laws of the human sentiments, a man has no right to do wrong, hence the moment he does a gross wrong he forfeits his liberty. I now quote from Prof. W. B. Powell on Human Temperaments:

"When, therefore, a man has been found to have injured society or the public by theft, burglary, robbery, murder, or in any other way, except by accident, the public safety requires that he shall be taken out of the community and kept out of it until a very probable certainty shall arise that when liberated he will not again transgress. And as the offender can be rendered useful to his family, his creditors, and his country, it would be a great outrage upon all these interests to destroy him. On the contrary, there is a preponderating motive to save him, more especially as he may be converted into a good citizen during his useful confinement.

"I have found it very difficult to make people understand in what respect this differs from punishment. Is it punishment to turn a man out of church because he will not live in conformity with its requisitions?

"Can this not be done without any more motive to punish him than is manifested toward a mortified leg when it is amputated to save the body? If society could have a certainty that the offender would go into the forest and live entirely removed from civilization, he should have the privilege of going, but this certainty can not be had. Let it be remembered that according to the laws of the human sentiments, no man has a right to liberty any longer than he acts in conformity with them; when, therefore, he infracts them by doing injury to others, he forfeits his liberty, and then, in point of natural law, he has no more right to it than he would have to a horse that he had stolen; and certainly no one would assert it to be punishment to take the horse from him."

But I must here differ a little with my brother. For although society might have no motive to punish a man by depriving him of his liberty, or by confining, working, and educating him for an indefinite time in a reformatory institution to which no disgrace would be attached, yet the bare circumstance of removing him from society and from his family would be, with a large majority of men, attended with considerable punishment, from the fact he is a social and affectionate being, and like all other animals, can not properly enjoy life out of his natural element, remote from his family, his relatives, his old neighbors, and the wide world to which he must be attached by natural ties. However, this punishment would be considered, even by the criminals themselves, as a necessary act of kindness for the protection of society and the reformation of the ignorant and deluded; therefore, it would almost cease to be punishment when compared to the unnatural and cruel manner in which they are now treated—throwing them into ignominious prisons and working them as any monster would work a brute, and giving no part of their wages to their destitute and worthy families—by fastening on them and their innocent but unfortunate families endless disgrace—by committing on them moral and physical murder.

But when the liberty of the offender has been taken into custody, it becomes the duty of the law to ascertain as to the fact whether he has or has not offended. If the affirmative shall be found to be the fact, the conclusion is certain that he should be removed from society, whether idiotic, sane, or insane—questions with which the court has nothing to do,

Justice has now been done to society; all its individuals may go to sleep under a feeling of security. The offender has been placed where he is to remain until he can come out with safety to the public good.

It is now proper that we should visit the prisoner, and ascertain his true condition, that justice, at least, should be done to him. An investigation of his condition discovers that he has not received such an education as would enable him to comprehend his relations to or his duties in society, or he has had entailed upon him an organization indicating such a deficiency of the human sentiments as to render it impossible that he should be a law unto himself, and that he has not been educated or trained to act in conformity with the established laws of society.

In either case it is evident that society was the first offender, and as a natural consequence it has suffered, and that the one through whom it was made to suffer has now to suffer in consequence of his act; and if punishment is to be introduced, society, for its neglect to the prisoner, deserves more than he—indeed, all of it.

In civilized countries the municipal laws and institutions are supposed to be founded upon the supremacy of the human sentiments, otherwise it is still in the animal or savage state, *which is unfortunately in a great degree the fact*. A society existing strictly under the supremacy of the human sentiments, would take care to prepare every individual for a life of harmony with its institutions, and in proportion as it neglects to do this, will it suffer through its neglected individuals? This is not all; a state of society long existing under the supremacy of the human sentiments could not furnish a degraded or criminally constituted individual any more than the cattle about Lexington, Kentucky, where proper attention has been given them for many years, can furnish a scrub cow or ox. Both ignorance and degradation are, therefore, referable to society, and all that it suffers through its evil-doers are consequences which as inevitably flow from the social infringement of the laws of the human sentiments, as broken bones do from the infraction of the laws of gravitation.

Under this state of the facts what shall be done? Justice answers: "Although the safety of society required that he should be taken out of it, yet it does not follow that our obligations to him are to be in this wise canceled. We should, as far as possible, make restitution for our neglect, not only to him, but to his ancestry. He should have our kindness and charity as an unfortunate individual of our race—as one upon whom the blighting influence of social neglect has fallen without any agency of his own. *We should provide for him kind and capable instructors, such as can convince him of the justice of his imprisonment—call into activity his human sentiments, and regulate by them the action of his animal impulses, and make him feel that society is kind and designs to restore him to liberty and happiness.*"

In other words, I have to say that inasmuch as all offenders are such because of inherited mental imperfection, an education at war with the safety and interests of society, mental deficiency, or mental derangement (insanity), they should be regarded as unfortunate rather than as criminal.

The laws, therefore, should furnish them protection, under such influences as will be favorable to their return to society, with a strong probability, not only of safety to the latter, but of usefulness.

To obtain these requisite results, our penitentiaries with proper modifications will answer; but the name should be changed; they should be called sanitary, or reformatory, or by some other name which conveys no idea of disgrace.

To the offenders every possible motive should always be presented that can favor reformation. As labor is indispensable to both health and happiness, they should be required to labor; but in this labor they should feel as much interest as they did in their labor before forfeiting their liberty; that is, all they can earn over and above the expenses of the institution should be placed to their credit, and subject to their order, under the discretion of the superintendent.

Unfortunately, I have again to differ with my brother in regard to the using of our penitentiaries for reformatory purposes; from the fact, a thousand years would not overcome the prejudice and scandal attached to such ignominious prisons—to such murder pens. Therefore, I would be in favor of erecting new and appropriate edifices on healthful and eligible sites, and also of tearing down all penitentiaries, not leaving one stone on top of another, that the coming generations may not behold the hateful relics of their ancestral folly and cruelty.

"The institution, morally and intellectually, should be under the guidance of one who, by talent and education, is capable of judging of the capacity, sanity, degradation, and degeneracy of each prisoner, and of treating each one accordingly; of awakening and directing the human sentiments; of training the animal propensities; of doing, in fine, all that can be done, promotive of their return to society. In a few words, this individual should be an educated, practical, and philanthropic phrenologist.

"Nothing like punishment should ever be inflicted. Whatever was requisite to do, to secure obedience, should follow as a necessary consequence upon violated law, as a broken arm succeeds to and depends upon a fall from a horse. Every prisoner should be made to believe that his removal from society was not for punishment, but for the protection of it; and this will be easily accomplished if the treatment that follow shall correspond with the idea.

"This course is essential, because the idea of punishment flows from and is received only by the animal faculties; and so long as they feel the imprisonment and the consequent treatment, so long will reformatory efforts be attended with a failure.

"Furthermore, everything that is done should be done kindly, and with an obvious intention to their advantage. By this means they will soon love and obey the officers, and feel grateful for the means which are bestowed upon them with a view to their ultimate liberty, happiness, and usefulness. The repose which this course would soon procure for their animal propensities, and the activity which their human sentiments would acquire, would in a short time render them more happy than they ever before had been.

"To an institution thus provided and governed, the laws should send every offender, not for a definite period, but for an indefinite one, or for a time as long as the safety of society shall require it. No one should be permitted to return to society before a strong presumption shall be obtained that he will be a good citizen. Under such a system from ten to fifteen, possibly twenty-five, per cent. would never be returned to society, and why should they? They are so nearly animals, that with enough to eat they become happy in the prison, but could not be happy out of it, because incapable of providing for their wants by any variety of consecutive industry.

"This is briefly my plan for the protection of society, and the education and reformation of offenders; and though the tendency of society is now toward an abandonment of punishment, although punishment has never adequately protected society, and although I am as confident that a plan in principle like this will ultimately be adopted by a more advanced civilization, yet a partiality for time-honored errors, a bigoted aversion to change, an existing love of vengeance, and the existing ignorance of the natural laws of man, will start a thousand objections to the plan."

To arrange two or three hundred offenders in a reformatory prison or institution, like the pupils of a college, in classes for moral and scientific study and instruction, and provide them with the necessary courses of studies from three or four teachers, as anticipated from the above plan, would be considered rather a startling novelty; yet a little reflection would show us that this suggestion is strictly practicable, and would be really economical. As the object of such confinement is not the infliction of suffering to gratify a revengeful spirit, but the protection of society and the general benefit and improvement of the public, it is certainly vastly cheaper to adopt any course of training for a reformatory purpose than to confine convicts under rigid and inhuman discipline, without moral and intellectual influences, and ultimately to send them forth upon the general country to repeat their career of crime, inflicting upon the communities not merely the outrages of robbery, arson, and murder, but the enormous expense of sustaining a profligate population, living by vice, and employing an extensive corps of police to prevent their crimes and to watch and arrest the criminals.

Education, which prevents crime, is vastly cheaper than penal law, which meets and punishes it; and even when that education has been in the first instance neglected, its beneficial effects may be realized by elevating the debased and restoring the harmony of a distorted character. Intelligence—the knowledge of ourselves, and hence of our fellow-men—of those great laws and influences which underlie and control all our actions—

necessarily tends to goodness; for, in proportion as the faculties of the mind become developed, it is able to discern what is the wisest course in life; what is our true and best interest (which is a bit of knowledge that not one in five hundred possesses); to discover that crime ends in misery, and that a virtuous life alone can yield much true enjoyment.

CHAPTER X.

PUNISHMENT FOR CHILDREN.

Do you think it wrong to punish children? "Spare the rod and spoil the child," you know.

This question was sent to me long ago for an answer in the laws of life. I have not replied heretofore, not because I have considered it of no importance, but, on the other hand, because of the immense importance which I attach to this subject, and because of my sense of incompetency fitly to discuss it.

I do think it wrong to whip children, if we give to the term "punishment" such significance as many people attach to it.

No parent may rightfully administer punishment to his child as a compensation or recompense for wrong committed—to wreak vengeance upon him or "pay him off" his evil doings. Yet I believe that oftener than otherwise parents do chastise their children with such motives. They possess the same notions about punishing children or criminals as they suppose God cherishes in his relations to men.

They think that if men are sinful God will arbitrarily send afflictions upon them in this world, or everlasting misery in another world, as a recompense, there being no natural connection between the sin and the suffering. I am not willing to think of God in that way. I believe that all suffering of men, whether in this life or in a future life, follows naturally and as a legitimate and inevitable consequence of sin committed, and that God, being true, holy, and loving, can not interfere to prevent the result. Suffering is born of sin.

If one is sick, it is because he or his ancestors have committed the sin of transgressing the laws of health, and the suffering naturally flows out of his transgression. God does not arbitrarily send it upon him to express his displeasure. If a little child dies, it is not an arbitrary act of God, taking vengeance or visiting judgment on the parent because of some moral obliquity or spiritual defection; but is the natural consequence of the physical sins (committed ignorantly perhaps) of the parent, just as truly as the withering of the bud on the rose-bush results from the gnawing of a worm at the root. If we are selfish and rebellious, hateful and hating one another, we must be dissatisfied and unhappy, because such consequences naturally flow from cherishing such vile spirits. God can not make a human being happy whose breast is the abode of demons. Such place *must be* foul and unclean. A distinguished preacher said not long ago, he is sure there is a hell, because he sees people in hell every day. But God does not put them there because he wants to wreak vengeance upon them, but because, whether they are in this world or in another world, the spirit which they entertain is one which comes from beneath—a selfish one. God has provided a means of cure for all the ills of humanity, but his remedy is not applied to the effect without removing the cause. It is a cure for sin, and thus it becomes a cure for the consequence of sin, which is suffering. If men will be shielded from the natural results of sin, they must depart from it.

The effect upon society, upon government, and upon individuals, would be salutary—quite reformatory—if men would reject the idea that God inflicts punishment arbitrarily; for then we should no longer punish criminals vengefully, nor would parents feel at liberty to *pay off* their children by inflicting suffering for offenses committed against them. They would never whip their children simply because they *deserve* it.

But if to punish is to *correct*, then are parents not only at liberty to punish their children, but they are bound to do so, provided they are well satisfied that the means used will accomplish the end sought, and provided also they can in no other way so well produce the desired effect. I presume that if all these considerations were well weighed in every case, three-fourths of all the punishment bestowed upon children would at once be abolished, and in the one-fourth of all the cases left, the parents would proceed to do their duty with great humility; for in almost every instance where it is necessary that a child should be punished, it is the parent's fault; or if not so, it is the fault of some person who has wronged the child.

If children were born with true and normal organizations and combinations of all their faculties, moral, mental, and physical, and were properly trained from birth, they would seldom need punishment. If there is a defective native organization, is it not the fault of the parents, or of their parents? If the training and education is not complete, is it not the fault of the parents or of others who influence the child? Children are born with bad tempers, with stubborn wills, with perverse propensities, some are born lambs, and some wolves or tigers, merely because the parents or grandparents are or were faulty in their development and culture, and if, instead of disciplining bad tempers in themselves, they set about punishing these in their children, should they not do it with self-abasement? The parents may have earnestly tried to do the best they could under their conditions and circumstances; but do their best, they can not prevent their children from inheriting, in some degree, the effects of their errors and follies.

If Rarey has taught men in large measure to dispense with whipping animals by instituting more rational management, why may not the principles of science be applied to children, in instituting improved methods of governing them, or rather of teaching them self-government, for this is the end always to be sought by discipline, whether it be of children or of criminals.

Not until the people learn that the world is to be improved, and Christianity is to find its greatest triumphs in the begetting and training of children under the controlling influences of love and wisdom, will they receive justice at the hands of those who have the charge of them. When that time comes, the welfare of children will not be made secondary to the comfort of self-indulgence of their elders, to the care of houses, lands, or shops, or to the demands of fashion.

They will not be begotten by accident and brought to the birth without reference to the laws of their being, and left to make their way in the world without any proper provision for the best discipline of mind and of body. Many a mother now worn and weary by her labor and care, irritated and fretted by the inquisitiveness and activity of her child, running riot for want of wise direction, hits the little one a slap over the ears, or seizes and shakes and spanks it, when, if she had the freedom which the care-taker of children ought to have, she could easily lead it in the right way without a blow or a harsh word. The necessity for punishing children exists by far more in the circumstances which surround them than in the natures or conditions of children themselves. A child neglected when it deserves and ought to have attention, becomes restive and ugly, and the mother, under pressure, feels compelled to punish it; whereas this might be avoided as well as not—yes, far better than not, insomuch as it is better to prevent a wrong than to correct it when it has once been committed. Many times children have to be punished because of bad bodily conditions, for which the parents are entirely to blame. A sickly, peevish child is much more likely to need correction than a healthy, happy one, and if the child is sick the parent is responsible. Many children are cross and unmanageable, and have to be subjected to punishment simply because they are fed upon flesh meats and condiments, which irritate and inflame the stomach, who, if they were restricted to simple and nutritious diet, taken with regularity at proper intervals, would be easily managed. Children become cross and have to be punished because their nervous systems are excited in innumerable ways, when they ought to be left quiet and undisturbed. I knew one mother whose only child was subject under any excitement to fits of intense anger, for the exhibition of which he would have received severe punishment at the hands of the majority of mothers.

But this woman adopted the practice of bathing soothingly the head of her child in cold water for half an hour whenever he became angry, which invariably had the effect to bring him to his right mind, to repentance, and reconciliation to her. If, then, parents feel called upon to administer punishment to their children, let them do it after due consideration, with humanity, and with a conviction that it is rendered necessary by the false conditions or circumstances in which the child has been placed. MISS H. N. AUSTIN.

Why blame the thistles for having grown,
After we ourselves the seed have sown?

KIND WORDS.

Kind words are dew-drops from the soul;
  The source is never dry;
For as we draw from that pure spring,
  'T is replenished from on high.
Oft have kind words saved from despair—
  Perhaps a drunkard's grave—
A brother, sister, or a friend,
  Whom naught else e'er could save.

Let no occasion ever pass
  To give a cheering word;
Each one is registered "On High,"
  The giver's prayers are heard.

The journey, from the cradle to
 The grave, is but a day;
None e'er should lose a moment's time
 Contending by the way.

But if a fellow-being fall,
 Or weary on the road,
Give him kind words to cheer him on,
 And bear with him his load.
E'en though your own be hard to bear,
 To you strength will be given;
For God rewards kind words and acts—
 They're stepping stones to heaven.

THE PRESS.

Firm in the right the daily press should be,
The tyrant's foe, the champion of the free;
Faithful and constant to its sacred trust—
Calm in its utterance, in its judgment just.

CHAPTER XI.

MOTHERS AND THEIR DAUGHTERS.

"SOME mothers are at fault in releasing their daughters from toil and care. By so doing they encourage them in indolence. The excuse these mothers sometimes plead is, 'My daughters are not strong.' But they take the sure course to make them weak and inefficient. Well-directed labor is just what they require to make them strong, vigorous, cheerful, happy, and courageous to meet the various trials with which this life is beset.

"Mothers, labor will not injure your daughters so much as indolence will. Do they feel weary at the close of their day's duties? A night's rest will refresh and invigorate them, and in the morning they will be prepared to engage again in useful labor.

"Many mothers are too ready to shield their delicate, ease-loving, pleasure-seeking daughters from care and responsibility, as though they feared a little care would injure them. These mothers make a sad mistake. In lifting responsibilities from their daughters, they make them inefficient for useful labor, and render them useless so far as practical life is concerned.

"Their education has a tendency to make them thoughtless of others. They are frivolous and, perhaps, vain. Their minds are occupied with themselves.

Their own amusements and selfish gratifications are their chief study; hence they become proud, unteachable, unamiable. They fancy themselves delicate in health, when they have the powers within them, if called into exercise, to make useful, working women.

"Indolence is a curse to them, as they learn the fashionable simpering and artificial lisping so common with spoiled young ladies. Affectation is seen in almost every action. They are amused with themselves, and are thoughtless of others. They live upon the plenty which surrounds them in their parental homes, and depend upon the bounty given them of their parents. They lean upon parental strength, and hence fail to acquire the power of depending upon themselves. And those of this class are unprepared for the stern realities of life. They make no provision for the losses and disappointments of this inconstant life. They may be deprived of property and of parents. What, then, will they lean upon? They have not acquired a principle of self-support, of noble independence and self-reliance, and they droop through murmuring, disappointment, and discouragement. They may then regret the defects in their education, and blame their mothers for them. These are some of the many fruits of a mother's mistaken fondness.

"Inactivity weakens the system. God made men and women to be active and useful. Nothing can increase the strength of the young like proper exercise of all the muscles in useful labor. But the indulgent mother frequently sacrifices her life in her misguided affection for her children. And are they, in any way, benefited by the great sacrifice of the precious strength of the mother? No; but they are positively and permanently injured. They are taught to think and care only for themselves—'are taught to be disobedient, ungrateful, extravagant, and worthless young women—unprepared to make good wives or good mothers—only fit to squander what they may inherit, and finally to become a disgrace to themselves and to their relatives.' 'Just as the twig is bent the tree inclines.'

"Mothers should instruct their daughters not to yield to indispositions and slight ailments. If they complain of inability to labor, they should not be urged to eat. They should be taught that if they are unable to perform light labor, the system is not in a condition to take care of food. They should fast for one or two meals, and drink only pure, soft water. The loss of a meal or two will enable the overburdened system to overcome slight indispositions, and even graver difficulties may be overcome by this simple process.

"It is very injurious for persons in full flesh to lie in bed simply because they feel sick. Some, even while thus inactive, eat regularly. The physical, mental, and moral powers are enfeebled by indolence.

"Mothers, if your daughters are surrounded with plenty, do not make this an excuse for neglecting to give them an education in the useful branches of household labor.

"Do not encourage them in indolence, or allow frivolous employment of their time. You should help your children to acquire a knowledge, that, if necessary, they could live by their own labor. You should teach them to be decided in following the calls of duty."

Now the foregoing suggestions and admonitions apply equally well to fathers and their sons, and all parents who may chance to peruse them might do well to— TAKE WARNING. Yes,

"A word to parents, one and all,
 Who in our city do reside;
See to your children, large or small;
 Instruct right, be this your pride.

"'T is wicked pride to dress in silk,
 And leave your children in the street;
The little ones need bread and milk,
 And larger ones their bread and meat.

"When left alone they run astray,
 Especially your darling boy;
Ye fathers do n't forget the way,
 It is to give your sons employ.

"For idleness is sure to bring,'
 Some trouble to them in the end;
And many in this town will swing,
 If in their ways they do not mend.

"Already some have had to go
 To learn a trade, and learn it free;
And where are others that we know?
 In prison? No, but ought to be!

"Ye mothers, too, pray do your part,
 And teach your daughters right to know;
When they 're old they 'll not depart,
 If train'd the way they ought to go.

"Your child was given you to rear,
    In ways of honesty and truth;
But ah! too plainly doth appear
    The sheer neglecting of the youth.

"If mothers take such frequent tramps
    Upon the streets, and children roam,
No wonder that your sons are scamps,
    Nor that your daughters *love not home.*

"Pigs, cows, and horses, where are they?
    Of course they'll not neglected be;
But where the children are to-day,
    You scarcely can take time to see.

"Now, if at once we will begin,
    According to the blessed Word,
We'll hear the welcome, enter in,
    And taste the joys of thy dear Lord."

CHAPTER XII.

MATTER AND MOTION.

I know of nothing in nature and the constitution of things which is not comprehended in *matter* and *motion*. Motion is change in opposition to a state of rest. Matter is material substance; but matter and motion are inseparable, insomuch that we can form no idea of the one in utter absence of the other. When we conceive of the existence of matter, it has form, and all forms are from motion.

We can conceive of a *force* as inherent in matter, which may become motion. Thus, of oxygen. It is so often, if not always, present in all changes in matter that it would seem to authorize the belief that this gas may be the force which is the germ of all motion. I speak of magnetic and electrical forces without implying actual motion; that is, any relative motion, any change in a given state. But then we must bear in mind that *motion* is as general and as extended as matter is, so that as we can not know what matter is, so we can never tell where motion's limits are.

Thus the motions of my hand now writing have been caused by an eternal series of motions that have gone before. Hence, although we may refer to any specific motion, and say it was first or last when compared with another change which went before, or which followed after, yet of all motions that have gone before, we could not say of one that it was first of all, in the sense of bearing a numerical relation as the first to all motions, past, present, and future.

It may be sufficient for our present purpose to say that certain motions depend on certain qualities and quantities of matter. But, at the same time, it is easy to see that these degrees in the qualities and quantities of matter are determined by motions which go before, so that it is manifestly true, as I have stated, the terms *matter* and *motion* comprehend all that we can know of anything.

When, therefore, we speak of the human body, and the laws of life or of health and disease, we can mean nothing more than is comprehended under these terms. What we want to know must have respect either to the quantity or qualities of the matter which enters into the composition of our bodies; and these involve also the idea of motion, which makes more or less of both the one and the other.

The term *quality* applies to motion as really as to matter, and we know that quality appertains to the inherent forces (positive and negative) in nature, as really as they distinguish the sexes in vegetable and animal life. Motions and qualities reciprocally induce each other, as we see in the case of heat; motion produces heat, and *vice versa*.

I do not say which may be first in the primal order of nature, whether heat or motion; but I know that in so far as motion is frictional, electricity is always evolved, so that all motion may be said to be more or less electrical;

that is, it produces electricity, or is produced by it, or both.

This much, then, premised, I proceed to observe that there are two great questions which meet us on the threshold of our general subject:

1. As it respects the elements which enter into the composition of the human body, their number, their qualities, and the proportions in which they are mixed or combined. These it is not difficult to determine, as by chemical analysis we know how many elements have thus far (64) been discovered in matter; and in the same manner we can ascertain how many are to be found in the composition of animal bodies.

2. As it respects the motions which make life and health. These are numerous and complicated. Thus we can understand in what sense the motions which form the oyster or a potato are low, or less complicated than those which make animal life in the form of a human body.

CHAPTER XIII.

PHILOSOPHY, MYSTERY, AND MUTATION.

REALLY how little one knows; with a universe before us we are yet striving to master the mysteries of an atom. Even to the question, what is an atom, philosophers preserve a modest silence. It is true that philosophers have been rewarded with the discovery of the law by which many atoms unite, but how small the discovery in proportion to what remains to be discovered! Surrounded by forces, philosophers are yet asking themselves the question, what is force? Contemplating the wonderful, the beautiful, the varied phenomena of nature, we ask, are all these phenomena the result of many forces? Or, is it one force which under all these different aspects is manifesting itself to our senses? Phenomena are ever changing; rocks crumble, rivers flow, sometimes they change their courses, sometimes they dry up altogether. Trees bloom, they wither; generations of men come into being, pass away to make room for others; change everywhere—rocks, rivers, flowers, oceans, mountains, trees, birds, beasts, and fishes; all change, ever did change, and always will.

But why do they change? What is it that does change them? Is there something under all these changes that remains, though invisible and intangible, ever the same—changing, but itself remaining unchanged? Who shall answer us? Philosophy presumes not to do it, nor ever to be wise above what is revealed. Philosophy observes these changes and notes the order of their occurrence, but beyond this it does little; it deals with the manner, it follows the method, it answers the "how" of a thing rather than the "why." Take, for instance, two gases, oxygen and hydrogen, neither of them fluid; they unite and water is formed. Philosophy will tell you how to unite them, but declines an answer to "why" water is formed by the union. The great reason why philosophers know more than others is that they observe more than others. A chemist knows what passes under his observation—he knows no more. Hypothesis and speculation begin where observation ends. Take the tiniest flower that grows on the road-side, take the buttercup or take the daisy, and ask philosophy to explain how each receives its own peculiar tint; take man, and ask philosophy whence he came; ask his history; ask how he came to be the wonderful being he is, endowed with life and motion, with aspirations and emotions; or ask why he is not other than he is. Ask what that wonderful thing is we call gravitation. We say that gravitation molds a tear and gives shape to a world. Gravitation causes a balloon to ascend and rain to descend; it holds the earth on its orbit, and is the universal bond of union, but what is it? Philosophy has never yet vouchsafed an answer. What is electricity? What is the magnetic fluid? What about the mysteries of a blade of grass—a fragile thread which yet grows upward and straight, despite the boisterous gales which so rudely over them blow? There are mysteries in every leaf, in every flower, in every stone upon which we tread. There are mysteries in every insect which dances through the hazy atmosphere; mysteries here, there, and everywhere. And what does philosophy say to all these mysteries? It says the solution of these mighty problems are hid deep down in the bosom of nature; make use of me as an instrument to interrogate her—she may yield up her secrets tardily. She may do it with a seeming unwillingness, but to him who perseveres in his asking shall some of the secrets be told. Are discoveries slow, philosophy must be patient; are nature's secrets but darkly revealed, philosophy waits for more light. Philosophy is earnest, persevering, yet cautious and modest. Where light is not vouchsafed, she utters no oracles; where darkness prevails, philosophy stands awaiting a higher altitude of the sun of science, and in proportion as light is given, she proceeds from conquest to conquest.

Therefore the following conclusion appears reasonable: That nature, throughout all nature and in all her ramifications, ever did, ever will, act like herself; and, judging from all we know, there can be no doubt of this fact.

Call it wisdom, call it power, call it fate, call it what you please, altering the name does not alter the thing. Let the universe, then, embracing all the heavenly and earthly bodies, move on in its course, for all things, though in everlasting conflict, worketh well, not only for the perpetuation, perfection, and harmony of all inert nature, but for the good of all animate creation. Yea, all those opposing forces, motions, and commotions—all those conflicting and warring elements in nature, morals, and politics—are nothing more than the agencies of the great *first* cause laboring incessantly to analyze and to purify the various elements; all necessary for our happiness and proper development.

And all striving for and tending to the great and universal law of equilibrium, which no sooner found than needs to be disturbed, to avoid inaction and consequent stagnation and ruin. Are not the heavens and earth sustained and kept in motion and harmony by their conflicting elements and opposing forces, by the laws of attraction and repulsion, by action and reaction.

Is there not an eternal warfare in every department of nature? The waters are forced to the mountain top to quickly return headlong, tearing, roaring, and dashing everything before them, until an equilibrium is found, which, no sooner done, than compelled to return to repeat the everlasting process. And the winds, too, by the action of heat and cold, forever contribute to keep up an irrepressible conflict in nature. Yes, kind readers, this sublunary paradise, this beautiful and fertile earth, has not escaped nature's immutable and irresistible laws; its every acre has been heaved and upheaved time and again, literally turned inside out. Vast rivers have disappeared and formed again in other localities. The seas have been heaved up into lofty mountains, and mountains become beds of seas. Onward! onward! is the language of all creation. The mountains lift up their heads and tell it to the clouds, the waters of the deep roar it up, the night winds whistle it, and the stars whisper it. Everything is onward in their formation and dissolution. Continents feel it and are convulsed with an earthquake. Cities hear its voice and rise into magnificence to soon disappear. Nations hear it and sink into the dust.

So everything is onward in formation, change, and perishability. The compact rock itself yields up its form and crumbles under the influence of heat, moisture, and frost; and the iron dug up from the recesses of the earth yields to the same laws of change.

Now if the works of nature thus obey the great laws of change, still more readily do the frail works of man yield to the same laws.

Witness the political and physical antiquity. Where is the old Assyrian empire, the earliest on the pages of authentic history—the empire of the great Cyrus—the Grecian empires and republics? And where is the hundred-gated Thebes—Babylon, the city of palaces—Jerusalem, the city of the chosen One? And where is Rome, called by her builders The Eternal? All, all, have yielded to the same law of mutation, and are numbered only among the things that have been.

Now if the law of change has worked such wonderful feats among the ancient nations—if their empires and republics, their fair fields and magnificent cities, have been overrun and desolated by contending armies—may not this proud republic expect sooner or later to experience like vicissitudes and calamities? Or is this boastful and young nation destined to form an exception to all those which have preceded it? No, no; we must not so deceive ourselves, for we, too, have sinned, are still sinning, oppressing the homeless, the weak, and destitute of all nations. Hence we, too, *must expect* that the day of retribution will come ; that this republic, too, with all its fair fields and magnificent cities will yet be overrun, desolated, and demolished—must also pass away and be only remembered among the things that have been.

CHAPTER XIV.

LAND MONOPOLY.

I now propose to devote a few lines to the all-important subject of land monopoly, hoping, by the time I am done with the subject, to convince the more thinking and liberal part of my readers that it is the chief cause of all those excesses of ignorance, poverty, servility, and crime found among men; that it demands, and ever has had, for its gratification and support a "divine institution;" that it is the origin, not only of all despotism, monarchy, war, and polygamy, but also of all slavery, either white or African. Hence those who oppose land reform do virtually encourage all the evils and vices known to human society.

Yet I am well aware that I have undertaken an arduous and fruitless task, and, perhaps, might as well amuse myself by riding on a broomstick through the ethereal regions; for it will be, I fear, as Dr. Combes says, in speaking of the difficulty of convincing the unthinking and prejudiced, "stubbing the thorns and enjoying no harvest," but as I am used to only a meager harvest, will not despair, particularly as I consider it my duty to contribute my mite toward bringing about so desirable a reformation, a reformation without which the masses never can be emancipated, enlightened, and elevated—without which we never can become a truly civilized and christian people. "Man first appeared naked in the tropical climes, where food was cultivated by the industrious hand of nature; but he soon clothed himself, and migrated to other crimes, being moved by the strong muscles and restless energies with which he was endowed. As soon as he advanced in civilization his connection with the products of the soil became more intimate; indeed, his individual possession of a certain spot of ground was made necessary so soon as he forsook the barbarian or migratory life and settled in permanent habitations.

"Previous to civilization, living, as he did, upon animal food and such fruits as nature presented without cultivation, he could roam with almost as much freedom as the beasts he hunted down for food and raiment. But after he settled in permanent homes, he was thrown more directly upon the resources of that labor which he might expend in cultivating the soil. It was then that the question of individual possession of the soil arose. It was then that every one felt the necessity of having a portion of the earth set apart and recognized as his exclusive possession."

It is, however, futile to speak of different states of society as manifesting more or less clearly the intimate connection of man with the soil; for all mankind, in all climes and conditions, are dependent upon the earth for food, raiment, and habitation. Man's connection with the soil is as intimate as the connection of the different organs of his own body. Separate but one vital organ, and the whole must perish. Sever man from the soil, make him an outcast from the earth, without a space that he can call his own, and he dies at once. He can not survive such violence, unless he be charitably taken under the roof, and bountifully fed upon the products of another man's labor. But only restore to him all his rights, and every one will rejoice in earning his own living, desiring no aid from, and ownig no thanks to aristocrats nor to ancestral estates.

Thus we find two great channels through which flow all the necessaries of life. These are land and labor; the former produces all things when the latter is made freely and efficiently to operate upon it. It, therefore, strikes the reader at once that the most intimate and harmonious relations should exist between these two vital agents of production for the sustentation of human life. It must follow that the least disturbance of these relations will produce, sooner or later, destructive consequences; for it is a law of nature that human life shall not be taken. It depends upon the food which grows of the soil, and it is an equally vital law that every one shall have an individual, independent, and inalienable interest in the soil. "He takes my life," says Shakespeare, "who takes the means whereby I live." He, therefore, who monopolizes the land, robs some one else of his natural interest in the land, and consequently of his means of support.

It is no palliation of this *crime* to say that there is land enough for all, even though I do take a thousand acres or several city lots. There is land enough, and always will be, under the land system of nature; but there is not land enough, even now, under the monopoly system of society. The soil should be dedicated to labor, and held sacred to its use alone. This is self-evident, for it meets the response of every head and every heart.

The land calls for labor, and labor cries out for land on which to expend its energies for a useful purpose. The land does not belong to labor under the present laws of man; for those who desire to work upon it are not freely permitted to do so according to the promptings and unmistakable suggestions of nature and justice. A price is put upon that which should no more have a pecuniary valuation than the air, the light, or the water. The naked man, as he comes from his Creator, has no means of paying a price, and therefore he is cut off from his natural connection with the soil; hence he can not be admitted to the bosom of his mother earth, nor permitted to labor on the soil until he has hired out his bones and muscles, sold their use to the landlord or capitalist for a consideration, and accumulated enough, from his forced labor under an absolute master or despot, to pay the price which the law and false circumstances have put upon the land.

This earth is not the product of human labor; it was not created by man; it was provided by the Author of Nature; it was not originally sold to any despot, or class of despots, by Almighty God, for and in consideration of the almighty dollar; it was made productive, and man was created to live upon its productions; it was adapted to the labor of man in dressing and cultivating it, and, therefore, in the order of nature, those who will labor should possess the earth; and as all should produce their own support in some way, all should have free access to a portion of the soil.

Therefore, it is obvious from the foregoing fact that every man and woman born into this world has as natural a right to food, raiment, education, and a fair share of the soil as they have to breath the common air, to drink of the cooling fountain, or to enjoy the genial rays of the sun, or as the wild deer and squirrel has to sip the waters of the mighty Mississippi or Amazon rivers. And the only reason why they are denied these inborn rights, is because the rich are allowed by mal-legislation to oppress the weak—is because the rich are allowed to prey upon the poor just as the wolf preys upon the innocent lambs.

From this exclusion of man from the soil, flow all servitude and slavery, all poverty and ignorance, all crime and misery, that can proceed from so fundamental and violent a breach in the system of nature and of God. The people are cast out from the earth and made pensioners on the bounty of the great monopolists, who wield their power by the force of legal wrong, of shrewd capacity, of unscrupulous conscience, thereby making labor unpleasant and repulsive.

It is well settled that all a man produces by his own toil is his property against the world, our late slave laws to the contrary notwithstanding; this is personal property, together with the improvements he may make on the land

The authors agree that labor founds the right of property in every state of society, and that according to natural law, labor is the only original way of acquiring property; that the land is one of the elements of production, indispensable to the efficiency of labor, and therefore is the original and natural property of labor. That is, the use of the land; for no one has a shadow of natural or just right to a foot of ground which he does not use. While he is in possession of a proper portion, it is his against the world; but when he forsakes it for another location his right to it is gone, and it then belongs to whoever may succeed him in its occupancy. This is the only true relation of man with the earth, and a recognition of this great principle is the only means of securing the use of the soil to all the people, and of making their labor far less, but yet more profitable, respectable, and pleasant.

The amount of labor now exacted to secure the necessaries of life is far greater, severer, and more protracted, day by day, than is demanded by the law of nature; hence that which otherwise would be a real and continual pleasure is made a source of pain; instead of being an object of delightful pursuit, it is one of almost constant and universal dread.

It should, therefore, be an object with all natural or political economists, as well as of all statesmen and philanthropists, to inquire into the causes of this depression of labor, and to direct the manner in which the natural and pleasurable order in this behalf may be restored.

Labor is the natural attraction by which man is drawn to the good and the true; and if this chain, which binds man to his destiny, to progress, and to happiness, be broken, the whole moral world must necessarily be deranged and confounded. Not less disastrous to the material world would it be to break the chain of gravitation which upholds the planetary system, than to invert the order of nature in the moral world. Order is maintained everywhere beyond the reach of man, and it is his duty to preserve it in the sphere of his own action.

But it might be asked by some of my readers, what first gave rise to this land monopoly? It originated in the feudal system, so-called, which prevailed about a thousand years ago among the barbarous nations—the Goths, Vandals, Huns, Lombards, etc., that overran the countries of Europe on the decline of the Roman empire. It was adopted eventually by most of the princes of Europe, and it is generally believed to have been first introduced into England by William the Conqueror.

When the barbarians alluded to had made a conquest of the provinces of the Roman empire, the conquered lands were distributed by lot; hence they were called *allotted* or *allodial*, and they were held in entire sovereignty by the different chieftains, without any other obligation existing between them than that of uniting, in case of war, for the common defense. The king, or captain-general, who led on his respective tribes to conquest, naturally received by far the largest portion of territory for his own share, and his principal followers, to whom he granted lands, bound themselves merely to render him military services. The example of the king was imitated by his courtiers, who distributed, under similar conditions, portions of their estates to their dependents. Thus a feudal kingdom became a military establishment, and had the appearance of a victorious army encamped under its officers in different parts of the country, each captain or baron considering himself independent of his sovereign except during a period of national war. Possessed of wide tracts of country, and residing generally at a great distance from the capital, these barons or lords erected strong and gloomy castles or fortresses in places of difficult access, and not only oppressed the people and slighted the civil majesty of the state, but were often in a condition to set the authority of the crown itself at defiance.

The fundamental principle of this system was, that the lands were originally granted out by the sovereign and were held of the crown. The grantor was called lord, and those to whom he made grants were styled his feudatories or vassals. As military service was the only burden to which the feudatories were subjected, this service was esteemed honorable, and the names of freeman and soldier were synonymous. The great mass of the people, who cultivated the soil, were styled serfs, or villeins, and were in a state of miserable servitude. They were not permitted to bear arms nor suffered to leave the estates of their lords. The feudal government, though well calculated for defense, was very defective in its provisions for the interior order of society.

A kingdom resembled a cluster of confederated states, under a common head, and though the barons or nobles owed a sort of allegiance to the king, yet when obedience was refused it could be enforced only by war. The bond of union being feeble, and the sources of discord numerous, a kingdom often exhibited a scene of anarchy, turbulence, and war; and such was, in fact, the state of Europe, with respect to interior government, from the seventh to the eleventh century.

And thus has the land, which the God of Nature consecrated to the use of man equally with the water and the air we breathe, been, in all ages of the world, perverted from its legitimate use and made the means of serfdom, anarchy, despotism, and of wars and rebellions too numerous to mention.

And, strange to tell, vast numbers of men claiming to be intelligent, moral, and religious still advocate the propriety of such an unnatural and barbarian system. Yes, barbarian from the fact it is just as cruel to degrade, enslave, imprison, rob, and starve men *now* as it was a thousand years ago.

As a further demonstration of the injustice and cruelty consequent upon such monopoly, just observe the following figures and facts—facts which are but common, in a greater or less degree, to all aristocratical and monarchial governments, and which must, as a natural consequence, soon be our condition:

"In Great Britain there is land enough for twice the population, but monopoly throws nine-tenths of the people out of all ownership of the soil. Some of the nobility own whole counties in England, Ireland, and Scotland. The dukes of Sutherland, Buccleugh, and others hold a despotic dominion over more land than several millions of the people need to make them comfortable and happy—millions who are miserable now in consequence of their monopoly. The first-named duke holds more than four millions of acres, and his numerous tenants, who toil to support his princely splendor, are forbidden to erect a church of their own on that wide domain! He is a high churchman, while his tenants are dissenters; and in this we see how land monopoly not only invades life and liberty, but freedom of thought and speech also. It requires no further argument to prove such monopoly one of the highest crimes—indeed, the crime of crimes."

It has frequently been claimed by man that all was created for his good, and I suppose such men as the above-mentioned dukes, and tens of thousands of others in every country, must think that all was made for their good.

> "While man exclaims, See all things for my use!
> See man for mine, replies the pampered goose.
> And just as short of reason he must fall
> Who thinks all made for one, not one for all."

Nor are the above quoted outrages confined to Europe alone, for great numbers of individuals in the United States hold from one to a hundred thousand acres. Can there be any justice in any one man possessing such vast quantities of land? Indeed, no one man has any more right to possess even five or ten farms than he has to so many wives; because the first party deprives very many of ever owning homes absolutely, while the latter would forever oblige many worthy men to live without companions; the one being guilty of land piracy, the other of wholesale adultery—both great crimes before God and all wise, just, and benevolent men.

Nevertheless, I am well aware that the reading public, as a general thing, has very little taste or interest in any such reformatory subjects, and that many of my readers will oppose me with the following (and many other) so-called arguments: That the poor and landless possess very little emulation, energy, and industry; that they are careless, idle, and wasteful, out of the reach of redemption; that the majority of them desire no homes, and that if we were to give them homes—were to divide to-morrow all the lands equally between them—in a short time more than the half of them would squander their shares and be as poor as ever.

All this may be true, to some extent, owing to their present perverted natures—the legitimate work of land monopoly—of its oppressing and degrading consequences; yet such objections amount to mere gas and subterfuge, unworthy of a scholar, as I shall certainly prove. Vast numbers of them are, to some extent, deficient in the higher attributes of our nature, such as acquisitiveness, emulation, self-esteem, veneration, order, etc. Hence they, by fixed and unvarying laws, seek their affinity, and consequently marry in and in, among themselves, transmitting on their unfortunate offspring their every quality; consequently, it would be even *unnatural* for them to be anything but just what they are. And it is an admitted fact in philosophy that like follows like; therefore, if we had been born of just such parents, and had had just such entailments fastened on us, and had been raised under the same set of circumstances and influences, we, our so-called intelligent, affluent, and noble selves, would have been just as poor, ignorant, and ignoble as they are—would have had no more desire for industry, emulation, order, distinction, science, refinement, and bountiful homes than they have.

Nor was it in the plan of Deity that all men should be born with the necessary business capacities to accumulate and retain property; that all should be born with avaricious, overreaching, and grasping dispositions; that all should belong to the iron-fingered-live-for-self-stock of bipeds. And it is well for society that we can not be so alike, as there would soon be an end to all invention, science, refinement, progress, and civilization, all for the want of such laborers and benefactors in the great field of humanity as our worthy school teachers, inventors, philosophers, authors, lecturers, journalists, mechanics, preachers, statesmen, etc. For, as a general thing, the latter class are men of limited means, whose noble and generous souls rise far above sordid avarice, refusing to live merely for themselves, but mostly for their race. And may God and all mankind bless, nourish, and protect all inventors and reformers, "for of such is the kingdom of heaven."

But society, like everything else, requires, and ever must have, a variety of grades and distinctions; men for all purposes and vocations; men of various and conflicting opinions upon all subjects. It being only the abuses and excesses of the above-named wrongs and misfortunes about which the writer is complaining, for after we all shall have labored diligently and unitedly in suppressing the evils in society—in limiting the lands so as to provide comfortable domiciles and education for the masses—still there will remain enough and too much poverty, ignorance, servility, and crime.

Nor is it possible for this poor and landless class to be ever reclaimed so long as the said causes shall continue to exist; no, never, until the people shall become more generally enlightened in regard to their proper relations to the soil and to society; in regard to their natural rights; and also in relation to those great laws and influences which underlie and control all their actions; never until they shall go to work in earnest by enacting laws, to take effect in fifteen or twenty years, limiting every man to a certain amount of our common inheritance, say two hundred acres, more or less, according to location, quality, etc. Hence, every thousand acres, which now only provides one home, would produce for all time five homes, and every ten thousand, which many individuals now hold, would make fifty homes. And before this humane and christian law could take effect all things would grow into proper shape, no person being robbed of his property, and the poor no more to groan under the heel of the landed monopolist, but left and blessed with all the necessary means to work out his own salvation; therefore, we don't propose to so divide the lands or to give them homes; we only insist that they enjoy their natural rights, by throwing around them the necessary protection, that they may soon rise to a higher and higher plane, no more to be the vassals of unfeeling landlords.

In short, we only propose to extend to them a friendly hand, and say, Brothers, arise, arise, and be men!

It is true these large estates do not, at the decease of the holders, descend by the laws of entailment as in Europe, yet it is a fact, as a very general thing, that one or two of the sons, or sons-in-law, soon overreach or cheat all the rest out of their portions, and hastily become even greater shirks than their fathers had been. And so it goes, and ever will go, from bad to worse, until some such system of land reform shall be adopted.

Yes, the rich must continue to grow richer and the poor poorer, until soon we will have an aristocracy of the hardest stripe; and then it is but a short and easy step to monarchy, and which is just as sure to soon overtake this boasting people as that to-morrow's sun will set; because land monopoly and republicanism are incompatible elements; consequently, our so-called republic is now but a practical aristocracy. Then why not do these things for the great cause of justice and humanity, for what advantage is this monopoly to any party in society? The children of wealthy parents are universally indulged in idleness and extravagance, and gaze upon the great estates of their fathers, as the travelers do the pyramids of Egypt, with joy and admiration, until they become completely paralyzed; disqualified, as a general rule, for any profitable and honorable business; often dissipated and reckless, only fit to squander what they may inherit, and finally, perhaps, become a public charge. And the crazed father, having been for the last twenty or thirty years driven under the cruel lash of avarice, has finally lost about all his humanity; for, generally, as a man's wealth expands his soul contracts. Yes,

"Many a man, for love of self,
To stuff his coffers, starves himself;
Labors, accumulates, and spares,
To lay up ruin for his heirs;
Grudges the poor their scanty dole;
Saves everything—except his soul!"

And the general country is badly injured; great numbers of avaricious and grasping nabobs wallowing in unnecessary wealth—living, many of them, in costly palaces, while multiplied thousands of poor and destitute citizens surround them, whiling away, in uncomfortable hovels, an irksome and ignominious servitude; vast tracts of wild and unimproved lands lying in and on the margins of hundreds of settlements, rendering it impossible to have good roads, mills, schools, meeting houses, etc., which are always so necessary to meet the great ends of civilization; the farms grown up in thorns and thistles, the transient occupants having no interest in keeping them in order, or in repairing roads, bridges, etc.; and the cities and towns all over stained with smoky and dilapidated houses, much to the annoyance of good citizens.

So you see, everybody, the poor and the rich, the wise and the unwise, are seriously injured by this legalized but nefarious system of land piracy. Yet, notwithstanding, we find tens of thousands of intelligent and worthy citizens, high and low, the landed and the landless, including about three-fourths of our ministers, opposing land reform as an institution unjust and demoralizing in its effects—calculated to paralyze energy and enterprise; contending, and vociferously exclaiming, that so soon as individuals should reach their zenith (in land), they would become measurably indolent and worthless; that society would soon retrograde for the want of proper stimulus. Now all this is mere quibble and sophistry, and only uttered by such as have never carefully examined the subject, or by those whose heads are unfortunately deformed with the development of acquisitiveness. For the masses would never more than reach the amount of land allowed them, and would be content with that, as we now find them; and who are naturally our most pious, orderly, tasty, honest, and liberal citizens. While the more energetic, enterprising and exalted minds would soar far above sordid avarice, and find new and more noble fields in which to labor. Their active and restless spirits could not find rest and comfort in doing nothing; but they would now go to work as industriously as ever, distinguishing themselves by doing good for their race, for the unborn generations.

Has man no higher destiny on this earth than to grind, degrade, enslave, drive, and starve his fellowman? To accumulate and hoard up like some of the common animals? Did the God of Nature create these far-seeing and energetic minds merely to inflict his people with ignorance, degradation, and suffering? No, no; but they were created to enlighten and sustain our race; to teach and to legislate for the people; to secure and maintain for them their inalienable and God-given rights to life, liberty, and the pursuit of happiness. Then only remove the unnatural and unholy obstruction, and such intelligent and noble minds will soon find and labor in their proper spheres.

But the monopolists and their unthinking friends demur against all this—against all experience, justice, and common sense—and nervously exclaim that any system of land reform would be impolitic, unjust, and cruel; would rob men of their rights.

They, like our late slaveholders, claim the right to be let alone while driving, degrading, and starving the poor but worthy citizens; while monopolizing, not only the land, but the minds and souls of men. And it is even so with our legalized, but insolent and soulless dram-sellers "of good moral character;" they too claim the right to be let alone; claim the right to debauch the husband, and to rob and starve the worthy mother and her helpless and destitute children; claim the right to demoralize and unchristianize the whole human family.

Therefore, if this monopoly, with all its above-named excesses of ignorance, poverty, debauchery, slavery, war, and polygamy, be not morally and religiously wrong, and incompatible with true civilization, with justice and equality, with friendship, love, and truth, then there can not be anything sinful or criminal in all human actions.

But the world is progressing; hence it is but a "green" philosopher who is not willing to wait—to wait a hundred, or even five hundred years.

CHAPTER XV.

THE GREAT ATLANTIC CABLE.

"Two mighty lands have shaken hands
   Across the deep, wide sea;
The world looks forward with new hope
   Of better times to be;
For, from our rocky headlands
   Unto the distant west,
Have sped the messengers of love
   From kind old England's breast.

"And from America to us
   Hath come the glad reply,
'We greet you from our heart of hearts,
   We hail the new-made tie;
We pledge again our loving troth,
   Which under heaven shall be
As steadfast as Monadnoc's cliffs,
   And deep as is the sea.'

Henceforth the east and west are bound
   By a new link of love;
And as to Noah's ark there came
   The olive-bearing dove,
So does this ocean telegraph,
   This manual of our day,
Give hopeful promise that the tide
   Of war shall ebb away.

No more, as in days of yore,
   Shall mountains keep apart;
No longer oceans sunder wide
   The human heart from heart;

For man hath grasped the thunderbolt,
  And made of it a slave
To do his errands o'er the land
  And underneath the wave.

"Stretch on, thou wonder-working wire;
  Stretch north, south, east, and west,
Deep down beneath the surging sea,
  High o'er the mountain's crest;
Stretch onward without stop or stay,
  All lands and oceans span,
Knitting with firmer, closer bonds
  Man to his brother man.

"Stretch still on, thou wondrous wire;
  Defy space and time;
Of all the mighty works of men,
  Thou art the most sublime.
On thee bright-eyed and joyous peace
  Her sweetest smile hath smiled,
For side and side thou bring'st again
  The mother and the child.

"Stretch on! Oh, may a blessing rest
  Upon this wondrous deed;
This conquest where no tears are shed,
  In which no victims bleed.
May no rude storm disturb thy rest,
  Nor quench the swift-winged fire
That comes and goes at our command
  Along thy wondrous wire.

"Long may'st thou bear the messages
  Of love from shore to shore,
And aid all good men in the cause
  Of Him whom we adore;
For thou art truly but a gift
  By the All-bounteous given;
The minds that thought, the hands that wrought,
  Were all bestowed by heaven."

Most of the shadows that cross our path through life are caused by our standing in our own light.

Sins are like circles in the water when a stone is thrown into it—one produces another.

Even a viper should be killed with the least possible pain; since this animal, so pernicious to man, did not provide for itself a hollow tooth, nor put poison at its root.

A man who sincerely worships any object which he mistakes for his God is no more wanting in piety than a debtor who pays off a forged order is deficient in honesty.

The dimensions of Noah's ark, as given by Prof. Hitchcock, are as follows: 450 feet long, 75 feet broad, and 45 feet high. Now zoologists estimate the number of the different species of animals and insects to be not less than 150,000—1,000 species of mammalia, 6,000 species of birds, 2,000 species of reptiles, and 120,000 species of insects.

Circumstances and influences furnish the seeds of good or evil, and man is but the soil in which they grow.

www.ingramcontent.com/pod-product-compliance
Lightning Source LLC
Chambersburg PA
CBHW031942230426
43672CB00010B/2016